111 QUESTIONS ON ISLAM

111 QUESTIONS ON ISLAM

SAMIR KHALIL SAMIR, S.J.
on Islam and the West

A Series of interviews conducted by
Giorgio Paolucci and Camille Eid

Edited and translated by
FATHER WAFIK NASRY, S.J.

Co-translator:
CLAUDIA CASTELLANI

IGNATIUS PRESS   SAN FRANCISCO

Original Italian edition:
Cento domande sull'Islam: Intervista a Samir Khalil Samir
Copyright © 2002 by Casa Editrice Marietti S.p.A., Genoa-Milan, Italy

Cover photograph:
The Hagia Sophia in Istanbul
©istockphoto/Bill Stamatis

Cover design by Roxanne Mei Lum

© 2008 by Ignatius Press, San Francisco
All rights reserved
ISBN 978-1-58617-155-1
Library of Congress Control Number 2006939361
Printed in the United States of America ∞

CONTENTS

II. Can Islam Change?

III. The Challenge of Human Rights

Appendices

Preface to the English Edition

It Is a Fact That Muslims Are Now Part of Western Society

Due to large-scale immigration to Europe and the Western nations from Muslim countries since World War II, Islam is no longer a distant, exotic religion. In fact, Muslims are present throughout Europe and in many parts of the United States. Demographers project that the number of American and European Muslims will increase in the immediate future.

At present, Europeans are dealing with the challenge of protecting their values while seeking a solution to the social ills of alienation, segregation, poverty, and terrorism associated with the Muslim immigrants. Europeans express concerns about the rapid development of Eurabia.

Since the terrorist attacks on the World Trade Center "Twin Towers" in New York City on September 11, 2001, Islamophobia has spread through the Western nations. The following pages were prepared to help readers understand three things:

1. how Muslims and Christians can coexist peacefully;
2. what are the causes for the deep unrest that pervades the entire Muslim world;
3. and what are the means to promote greater dialogue and understanding between Muslims and Christians that will lead to a joint social, universal, and political effort for the benefit of all people.

In order to remain sensitive to and balanced in discussing the past and present situation, a question-and-answer format is used. The author responds to a series of questions posed by two journalists, one Italian and the other Lebanese. The intent of this balanced approach is to offer readers a clear portrait of Islam.

Muslims and Christians: How to Live Together

Islam shares some common elements with Christianity but also has many differences. The Muslim culture is quite different from that which emerged in the Western world as a result of the influence of Christianity. Because of massive demographic movement, both groups are now obliged to live together in contemporary society.

The Muslim world today faces one of the most profound identity crises in its entire existence. Comprising nearly 1.5 billion people living on all continents, it is struggling to find a common position for all Muslims. The search for identity has become particularly acute since the abolition of the khalifate (the office of Muhammed's successor, as head of Islam) on March 3, 1924, by Kemal Atatürk. The khalifate was the last representative symbol of unity of all Muslims. Therefore, contemporary Islam has no single recognized authority that would accomplish Muslim unity.

What are the foundations of Islamic faith? Why does Islam seem to be growing so fast today? What is the true meaning of the word *jihād*, in the Qur'ān and Islamic tradition, and in modern Arabic? Is it correct to say that men are superior to women in Islam, or is it just a cliché? Does religious freedom exist in Islam?

Furthermore, how does the Qur'ān present the life of Jesus? What is the Qur'ān's view of Mary? And of Christians and Jews? And of other religions? Is Islam a religion of peace, or one of violence? Can we reconcile Islam with democracy and modernity? Can we reinterpret the Qur'ān for our era? Does Islam distinguish between politics and religion?

Modernity Is Difficult to Accept

After having passed through centuries of stagnation, the Muslim world is experiencing great difficulty in facing modernity. The Christian world has had the leisure of several centuries since the Renaissance and the Enlightenment, since the French and American revolutions, and since industrialization to assimilate modernity slowly. Modernity is a concept that is foreign to many Muslims. This is exacerbated due to the fact that most Muslim countries suffer from widespread illiteracy and are governed by authoritarian political regimes or dictatorships. The concept of "human rights" is foreign to a large segment of the population.

There is an additional psychological barrier to accepting modernity. Many Muslim countries have experienced diverse forms of European colonization over the past two centuries. As a result, their attitude toward the West, modernity's birthplace, is ambiguous. This is a mixed attitude, one of simultaneous attraction and rejection. Moreover, because the West has become increasingly secularized in modern times, that is, rejecting many ethical principles and values that were common to both peoples, modernity appears to Muslims as a breeding ground for atheism and immorality.

Finally, the memory of the glorious period of the Middle Ages, especially between the ninth and twelfth centuries, when intellectual and scientific activities in the Muslim world had peaked and actually exceeded the achievements of the West, makes the current scientific and intellectual decline even more difficult to accept.

The Seeds of the Malaise

This current state of malaise results from the very sources of the Muslim faith: the Qur'ān, the *sunna* (Islamic traditions connected to Muhammad), and tradition.

Many Westerners fear Islam as a "religion of violence". Muslims often call simultaneously for tolerance and understanding as well as for violence and aggression. In fact, both options are present in the Qur'ān and the *sunna*. These are two legitimate manners—two distinct ways to interpret, to understand, and to live Islam. It is up to the individual Muslim to decide what he wants Islam to be.

It is necessary that we return to the very sources of the Muslim faith (the Qur'ān and the *sunna*) and proceed rapidly through history until we arrive at this very day. This book, therefore, aims at presenting the Islamic faith in an objective manner, at providing a sure knowledge of this faith, and at helping people to engage in a profound reflection from a double point of view: that of history and that of modernity.

To Live and Build the Future Together

This volume intends to promote understanding and encounters between Muslims and Christians. It aims to provide the groundwork for dialogue, in the true meaning of the word, not as a search for some compromise between these two worlds but in a sincere and unswerving commitment to truth, with openness to the other side. Ambiguous speech serves neither Muslims nor Christians but creates only more confusion. The commentary shows that both of these cultural and religious traditions have many things in common, as well as many differences. Accepting the differences of another group does not mean surrendering one's human, spiritual, or religious convictions.

Muslims and Christians can surely live together if they want to do so. Neither group has to give up its identity, dogma, or faith, because at that level no compromise is possible. As the Muslims' prophet says in the Qur'ān: "You have your religion and I have mine!" (Q 109:6).

Building a society together is certainly possible but also demanding, and that is precisely why it is worthwhile and rewarding!

Living together in a preexistent sociopolitical system means to accept the given system as it is but to remain open to improvement. This is the only way to grow together in wisdom and humanity and to build a future world open to everyone.

SAMIR KHALIL SAMIR, S.J.
and WAFIK NASRY, S.J.

Preface

This book results from a series of extended conversations between an internationally known expert on Islam and two journalists who have dedicated themselves for many years to studying key themes of Islam and analyzing the coexistence between people of different faiths and cultures. This volume does not presume to illustrate exhaustively the composite and complex reality that is the Muslim world. Rather, it endeavors to answer in an original way a series of questions about Islam that have been of popular interest for many years and more recently have acquired urgent importance following the September 11, 2001, attack on the World Trade Center "Twin Towers" buildings in New York City and the ensuing conflict in Afghanistan and Iraq.

Today there exists in the Western nations a desire for greater knowledge of a Muslim world that has already met the West both inside and outside their common borders for over thirteen centuries. Muslims and the entire Muslim world are still regarded with suspicion and distrust, which stem from a superficial knowledge of history and from an emotional reaction to recent political events.

Many western Europeans and North Americans conceive religious faith as something that belongs only to the spiritual dimension of life. As a result, Islam appears as a new and perhaps incomprehensible phenomenon because it proposes itself as a single composite unit, *dīn wa dunya wa dawla* (religion, society, and state). All-inclusive, Islam incorporates both the private and public dimensions of life into a single, grand reality, and it summons all the faithful into the *umma* (the community). At present, the Islamic *umma* is a community formed by 1.2 billion people. Islam definitely is a composite and complex reality. It has multiple groups and subgroups that contain many common characteristics with respect to rituals as well as approaches to reality and patterns of behavior.

This book's first chapter presents some considerations of the historical and cultural context into which Islam was born and in which it began its rapid expansion. Today an elementary knowledge of these aspects remains fundamental to any real understanding of Islam in all its complexity. The next two chapters deal with some of the main problems that Muslims have confronted over many centuries and still face today. These problems include the interpretation of holy books, authority, human rights, the condition of women, religious freedom, violence, and the relationship with modernity and with the West. The book's final two chapters examine some of the problems connected with the presence of Muslim communities throughout Europe, particularly in Italian cities, and some commentary about the present state of coexistence between Christians and Muslims. Such coexistence must be shaped without the prejudice and naïveté that have characterized recent interfaith dialogue and discussions on social integration.

Coexistence is a difficult building to construct even when people speak the same language and share the same values. It is a far more difficult goal to achieve when people belong to completely different worlds, even if they share common borders. A necessary condition for learning to coexist is a readiness to know other people. This is a necessary prerequisite for beginning an adventure, a prerequisite that often compels an individual to look in the mirror and rediscover the integrity and strength of his own identity. The Centro di Studi sull'Ecumenismo, from which this book originates, ideally strives to occupy the middle ground between the knowledge of the "other" and the rediscovery of one's own identity.

The expert guide for this exploration of the Islamic world is Samir Khalil Samir, a Jesuit priest of Egyptian and Italian descent whose academic biography shows his intellectual pedigree. Born in Cairo in 1938 and educated in France and the Netherlands, he now lives in Beirut, where he teaches in several departments of Saint Joseph University and where he founded CEDRAC (Centre de documentation et de recherches arabes chrétiennes [Center of Arabic Christian Documentation and Studies]). He has been a visiting professor at the University of Cairo (Egypt); at Sophia University in Tokyo (Japan); at Georgetown University in Washington, D.C. (United States); and at the universities of Graz (Austria), Bethlehem (Palestine), and Turin (Italy). He promotes and directs the publication of the collection *Patrimoine arabe chrétien* (Arabic Christian Heritage), which he initiated in Cairo and has continued in Beirut. Twenty-three volumes of this series have been published since 1978. He is the codirector of the review on Eastern studies *Parole de l'Orient* (Eastern Word) published in Lebanon. In Italy, he is founder and director (since 1994) of the Italian collection *Patrimonio culturale arabo cristiano* (Arabic Christian Cultural Heritage). He is the president of the International Association for Christian Arabic Studies and is the author of twenty volumes and around five hundred scholarly articles concerning Islam and the Christian East.

The above is only a small portion of the long and complex résumé of Samir Khalil Samir, but it would be a mistake to consider him a mere scholar who looks only at the objects of his research with the detachment of a refined intellectual. What is striking about his personality is that his knowledge of the topic is always accompanied by a passion for humanity—a thirst for the truth that resides in every person and that the scholar is capable of discovering and expressing in words. Part of the reason for this passion is that he belongs to the Arab-Christian world, a population that historically has been and is still today a crossroad of cultures and faiths. The Arab-Christian community is a relatively small world that preserves the memory of centuries of coexistence with Islam. It is full of contrasts and tribulations but not lacking in positive aspects. The Arab-Christian experience may represent a precious resource and paradigm for those in the Western world who today wonder how they can learn to coexist peacefully with Muslims who have emigrated from their countries of origin to settle in the West.

To the questions posed by the journalists, Samir Khalil Samir gives answers that may sometimes seem unpopular or in any case far from the mainstream opinion that has been accepted for years. His answers originate both from his profound knowledge of Islamic traditions and thought and from the familiarity he developed with the Italian immigration situation during his numerous academic sojourns in Italy.

The interview style, in question-and-answer format, allocates more exposition of content, conserves a colloquial atmosphere, and allows the scholar to enrich answers with anecdotes derived from his eventful life. The tone and vivacity of the comments—typical of Samir's homeland and people—have been retained as much as possible. Aware that the topics taken into consideration can easily inflame and divide public opinion, we did not intend to hide or soften them or adopt a "politically correct" way of speaking about the relationship between different cultures and faiths. All of the ideas expressed in the following pages were recorded with the intention of laying the groundwork for the growth of a peaceful coexistence with our new Muslim neighbors.

Conscious of the limitations of our work, we hope to have made available for a large public audience, more than for the many experts on the topic, a useful instrument for gaining a basic knowledge about Islam, its history, and the global reality to which our new neighbors belong.

Giorgio Paolucci and Camille Eid

Pronunciation Guide for Transliterated Arabic Words

’   indicates a suspension in the pronunciation
ḍ   emphatic *d*
dh   like *th* in English *the*
h   like *h* in *hotel*
ḥ   very aspirated *h*
j   like *j* in French *jeune*
kh   like *ch* in German *Buch*
q   emphatic *k*
ṣ   emphatic *s*
sh   like *sh* in *shop*
ṭ   emphatic *t*
th   like *th* in English *thief*
z   like *s* in *soup*
ẓ   emphatic *z*
ᶜ   guttural consonant close to the vowel *a*

A horizontal mark over *a*, *i*, and *u* (*ā*, *ī*, *ū*) means an extension of the vowel.

111 QUESTIONS ON ISLAM

I. The Foundations

A. Muhammad and the Birth of Islam

1. *To understand Islam, it is necessary to look at its origins. Would you please describe the social and religious context in which Muhammad's preaching began?*

Islam originated and developed in the Arabic peninsula, precisely in two principal cities, Mecca and Medina, between A.D. 610 and 632. These twenty-two years deeply mark, first, the history of Arabia, and, second, the history of the Middle East and the whole world, thanks to the extraordinary personality of Muhammad.

Born in Mecca around the year 570, Muhammad, whose father died just before his birth, lost his mother at a tender young age and was then adopted first by his grandfather and later by his uncle, members of the important tribe of Quraysh. Later on, he worked for Khadīja, a rich widow dealing in caravan trade goods. Later still, they were married.[1] At about age forty, in the year 610, following a period of solitary retreat in the mountains, he had an intense mystical experience and decided to dedicate his life to making everybody know the only God. According to Muslim tradition, at the time of Muhammad, many were looking for a monotheistic religion and a faith characterized by a strong

[1] Muhammad was twenty-five when he married Khadīja, who was forty.

31

spirituality. One of these persons, in particular, was Khad-īja's cousin, Waraqa ibn Nawfal, who had an essential role in the birth of Islam, as well as in the so-called *hanīf*.[2] Nawfal was an important source of information regarding monotheism.

These monotheistic ideas had a strong influence on Muhammad and transformed his existence to the point that he felt compelled to communicate what he felt mysteriously being revealed to him of occasion. The pagan environment in Arabia, in a certain sense, was predisposed to accept a monotheistic preaching, because many Jewish and Christian tribes lived in Arabia. Indeed, the only three Arab kingdoms known before or during the rise of Islam were Christian.[3]

What did Muhammad preach? In Mecca, the message was clear, simple, and markedly religious: believe in one God, Allah, and in the Day of Judgment, when everyone will be evaluated according to his actions and be sent either to hell or to heaven; implore from God the pardon of one's sins; pray the prescribed prayer twice a day (in the morning and in the evening);[4] stay away from adultery; and abandon the Arabic custom of burying newborn girls alive. Moreover, he preached social justice toward the widow, the orphan, and the poor through a detachment from riches, with undertones reminiscent of the prophet Amos in the Hebrew Old Testament. Above all, Muhammad declared that he was the prophet chosen by God to communicate to humanity the

[2] The word *hanīf* comes from the Syriac *hanpe*. For the Christian Arabs, it meant "pagan". In the Muslim tradition, however, the term acquires the meaning of a "monotheist" or "pure believer" who belongs neither to Judaism nor Christianity, and it is therefore applied to Abraham (cf. Qur'ān 3:67).

[3] The Himyarite kingdom in sixth-century Yemen and the two kingdoms of Lakhmids and Ghassanids in the north.

[4] Only later, in Medina, did the times for prayer become three (with the addition of one at noon); eventually they reached the present five times daily.

ultimate revelation, which had been transmitted to him through the Archangel Gabriel.

In his moments of intense isolation, Muhammad looked for support from the faithful of the monotheist religions. These were the Jews and Christians he called "the people of the Book", as they were the only ones who had a revealed book.[5] In most theological areas, they agreed with Muhammad's ideas with regard to monotheism, the revealed doctrine of the Last Day, and the resurrection of the dead, but they absolutely refused to believe his claim to be a prophet from God.

2.   *You say that Christians and Jews believe in the one and only God. Should we then infer that Allah is not a specific Muslim god, as many people in the West believe?*

Unfortunately this conviction is very widespread in Europe. Allah is not an "invention" of Muhammad or of the Islamic religion. The root of the word is common to all Semitic languages and those of the southern Mediterranean populations, and we find it in the Old Testament in the Jewish word *Elohim*, and also in Syriac and in Aramaic. The Arabic language offers the possibility of distinguishing between *ilāh*, god with a small *g*, and *Allāh*, the absolute God, where the Arabic article *al* was absorbed by the noun *ilāh*. So Allah was simply the name that the Arabs used to identify God, and Islam simply adopted a word that preexisted its birth and was already present in pre-Islamic poetry written by Christian authors.

The significant fact is that when Muslims translate the Qur'ān into the Western languages, some refuse to translate

---

[5] This expression is understandable only in the context of the Qur'ān. It cannot be accurately applied to Christianity. Christianity has never been presented as a "religion of the Book" but as the revelation of Christ, a revelation *also* delivered through books.

Allāh as *Dio*, or *Dieu*, or *God*. The habit of keeping the word *Allāh* in Arabic has become almost dogma today. I believe this practice evidences a fanatical attitude that claims that the name Allah defines the "Muslim God" and that no one else has the right to use it. In Malaysia, as a matter of fact, this absurd mentality led to the promulgation of a law that forbids Christians to use the word "Allah" to indicate God. The term is obviously presumed a Muslim monopoly. It is surprising that many Westerners, including the Italians, also follow this rule. They speak negatively about Allah, as a means to criticize Muslims. They act as if Allah were a divinity that belongs solely to Islam.

Allah was a part of the Arab pantheon, and many Arabs of the pre-Islamic period, among whom was Muhammad's father, were called *'Abd Allāh*, slave of Allah. It is possible that the pagan Arabs used the word *Allāh* to indicate a particularly powerful divinity, sometimes with the attribute of *al-Rahmān*, the Clement. Arab Jews and Christians employed the word *al-Rahmān* to indicate the only God, as revealed by some inscriptions of the pre-Islamic period discovered in Arabia. One very significant inscription dates back to the sixth century and contains a trinitarian affirmation, presenting *al-Rahmān* as the attribute of God the Father for the Christians, as it talks about *al-Rahmān*, his son *Christos*, and the Holy Spirit. *Rahmān* is therefore the fatherly attribute in the Christian tradition and the essential attribute of God for the Jews, while it was considered as one of the most powerful gods by the pagan Arabs.

3.   *How was Muhammad's monotheistic preaching accepted by the pagan population in Mecca?*

At the beginning, Muhammad's ideas did not encounter strong opposition from the pagan inhabitants of his city because they simply mocked him, accusing him of being possessed by some evil spirit or of being a fortune-teller. It is clear that Muhammad did not want to establish a new religion but simply wanted to admonish the Arabs about the forthcoming Day of Judgment; he pointed out more than once that religion is "one" from the beginning of creation and that he is the "seal" of the prophets (*khātam al-nabiyyīn*). Apart from a small group of young people of very modest economic conditions, few followed him.

However, when he openly began to attack the polytheism of his fellow citizens, opposition became stronger. His teachings threatened the interests of the local clans, who grew rich thanks to the pilgrims who visited the city every year. Mecca was, in fact, not only an important political, social, and commercial center in Arabia, but also a religious place. Already in the pre-Islamic period, all the tribes gathered there in a particular month devoted to the annual pilgrimage to worship their gods, which were placed around the Kaʿba (a cubical building that contains the "black stone", where Abraham was said to have erected an altar to God, according to Muslim tradition). During this time, the people would sell their goods and participate in poetry contests. Obliging these people to destroy their idols would have ruined their business.

Muhammad's preaching also irritated the inhabitants of Mecca and was rejected by them because it demanded solidarity with the poor. From this rejection experience, he derived the conviction that he was a prophet, opposed like all those who came before him, according to the proverb "A prophet is not without honor except in his own country and in his own house" (Mt 13:57b). Because opposition also came from his powerful Quraysh tribe, Muhammad felt even more isolated with his humble followers. Hostility against him led him to send his followers for some time into Ethiopia, a Christian kingdom, where they were welcomed with great generosity. It is related that the negus of Ethiopia, listening to the translation of the beautiful qur'ānic verses of the Annunciation, was moved and called his Muslim guests "brothers".[6]

4. *To the kingdom of Ethiopia was the destination of the first* hegira *(emigration), but there was another, more decisive one from Mecca to Yathrib.*

The growing opposition of the Meccans pressed Muhammad to modify his strategy. He reached an agreement with the rival city of Yathrib, the second most important city in Arabia, about 350 kilometers from Mecca. The inhabitants of Yathrib confirmed that they were ready to receive him, and he sent his followers there in small groups to avoid drawing attention: this was, in fact, a real betrayal of his city. He himself fled to Yathrib in the night, sometime between July 15 and 16 of the year A.D. 622, which marks the beginning of the Muslim calendar.[7]

In Yathrib, from then on named Medina,[8] Muhammad made agreements with all the local tribes, including the powerful Jewish tribes, and he began to organize the civil and religious life. In this city, he was finally free to realize his global project, which was religious, social, and political in scope. This evolution is the basis of the modern debate between Muslims about which version of Islam must be considered the true one: that of the first period, developed

[6] Cf. Qur'ān, Mary, sura 19. (A sura is a chapter in the Qur'ān.)

[7] The root of the word *hegira* is the same as that of Hagar, Abraham's servant girl who was obliged to flee into the desert with her son, Ishmael, who is considered the forebear of the Arabs. *Hegira* is capitalized when referring to the immigration to Medina (Yathrib). Muslims refer to the year *x* of Hegira.

[8] Abbreviation of *Madīnat al-nabī*, "the city of the prophet".

in Mecca and characterized by a strong spiritual aspect, or that of the second period, in Medina, with a strongly social and political nature. These are two very different conceptions.

5. *The two conceptions are different in the sense that the prophet also became a legislator and a leader?*

It should be remembered that Muhammad arrived in Medina with a small group of followers uprooted from their land and jobless, and they all needed money and assistance. His men were supported by those people who offered hospitality to them. Therefore, he tried to obtain the support of the Jewish tribes, the richest in the city, orienting prayers at the beginning toward Jerusalem and imposing fasting on the day of Kippūr, as Jews do. But his efforts failed, and the Jews did not recognize him as a prophet.

So around a year and a half later, he decided to change direction: prayer was oriented toward Mecca, and fasting was extended to an entire month chosen from among the sacred months of the Arab calendar. The new orientation of prayer (the new *qibla*) was destined to "conquer" the pagan Arabs. The fasting period no longer coincided with the Jewish fast, which was based on a solar calendar, but followed the Arab lunar calendar, which consisted of 355 days.

6. *After the break from Mecca, how did Muhammad provide sustenance for his followers?*

He resorted to raiding, *ghazwat* in Arabic. According to Ibn Hishām's most authoritative biography, titled *Sīra*,[9]

___

[9] Ibn Hishām (d. 834) based his account on Ibn Ishāq's lost *Sīra*, written around 750.

Muhammad was responsible for nineteen raids and pillagings during the decade spent in Medina.

Arabs of the pre-Islamic period observed two different seasons, totaling four sacred months, during which all warfare was banned. The tribes were permitted to fight during the other months of the year. Muhammad respected this legal custom. As a result, Muslims did not find anything incompatible between their traditional practices and their new faith. In short, war was part and parcel of the Bedouin culture.

The raids and pillaging provided Muhammad with rich spoils,[10] but they especially allowed him to construct agreements with different tribes in order to break out of his isolation and enlarge his base of followers. When he was in a position of strength, he attacked a new tribe, subdued it, and obliged it to pay a tribute; when he considered himself as strong as his enemy, he reached an agreement with him; when he felt he was in the weaker position, he simply avoided all conflict. Thus, thanks to his intelligent strategy, he managed to increase his base of followers and his economic support. As a consequence, the influence of Islam began to be felt numerically and politically in the Arab region.

During this period, he launched several raids against Mecca; in 624 he won the famous battle of Badr against Abū Sufyān's[11] caravan. On other occasions as well, he organized attacks against the convoys of Meccan merchants, but this tactic was too hazardous: during one of these raids, at

[10] Many suras talk about Muhammad's right to one-fifth of the spoils: "They ask you about the spoils. Say: 'The spoils belong to God and the Apostle ... obey God and His apostle, if you are true believers'" (the Spoils, sura 8:1); "Know that one-fifth of your spoils shall belong to God, the Apostle, the Apostle's kinsfolk" (ibid., 8:41).

[11] Prominent citizen in Mecca and the father of Moʿāwiya, the ancestor of Umayyad's dynasty (661–750).

the battle of Uḥud, he was injured and feared for his life. This episode, however, is claimed by Muslims as one of Muhammad's victories because the Meccans could have killed him, but they did not do it. This interpretation is confirmed by a passage in the Qur'ān.[12]

Muhammad, at this point, felt strong enough to attack the Arab Jews. One after the other, the three Jewish tribes of Medina were expelled from the city, and their properties were confiscated by Muslims. Then at the battle of Khaybar, an oasis not far from Medina where some Jews had taken refuge, the Jews were defeated by Muhammad's force after a long siege that lasted forty-five days. The victory at Khaybar entered Muslim mythology as sure proof of the superiority of Islam over the Jews. In fact, even today it is evoked in the slogans of Muslim militants and by the young people of the Palestinian *Intifada*.[13]

7.   *Did Muhammad continue with this strategy until the final battle at Mecca?*

After enlarging their membership base and becoming richer and stronger than any other Arab tribe, Muslims were finally able directly to attack Mecca. In January 630, Muhammad was able to enter the city of his birth without bloodshed, for the inhabitants recognized his military supremacy. He acted generously with his former fellow citizens (only three men and two women were condemned to death), but he demanded the destruction of all the idols around the Kaʿba.

[12] The ʿImrāns, sura 3:118–29, 139–60, 165–80.

[13] *Intifada* literally means "shaking off". In the context of the Palestinian-Israeli conflict, it means "to set free from Israeli oppression". The first intifada started on December 8, 1987, when four Palestinian men were crushed to death by an Israeli army transport vehicle. The second was on Sept. 28, 2000, when Ariel Sharon, with two thousand Israeli soldiers desecrated al-Aqsa Mosque and killed four people.

At this point, almost the entire Arabic peninsula was converted to Islam. Note that I said "converted to Islam", because
in reality it seems to have been only a form of military submission. In fact, the two things were the same because those
who submitted to Muhammad recognized him not only as a
ruler but also as a prophet sent by God. Political and military
submission was required, as well as the acknowledgment of
the only God and of his prophet. This acknowledgment
required a tribute payment for the maintenance of the army.

In March 632, the tenth year of Hegira, Muhammad could
finally make his first (and last) pilgrimage to Muslim Mecca.
The event became known as the Farewell Pilgrimage. During a speech before his Muslim followers, Muhammad communicated to the people the last received verse of the Qur'ān:
"This day I have perfected your religion for you and completed My favor to you. I have chosen Islām to be your faith." [14]
In May of the same year, while he was preparing a raid against
tribes in Transjordan, he got sick and was obliged to give up
the attack. His illness worsened, and he died a few weeks
later, on June 8, in the arms of his favorite wife, 'Aisha. [15]

B. Is the Qur'ān the "Uncreated" Word of God?

8.   *Let us examine more closely the figure of Muhammad the
legislator and preacher to determine how the Qur'ān was born.*

Muhammad worked hard to develop legislation for the
Bedouins, who did not have laws other than those transmitted
by tradition. In Medina, he had to solve a series of problems of

[14] The Table, sura 5:3.

[15] A monogamist during Khadīja's lifetime, Muhammad later had at least
another ten wives. He married 'Aisha, the daughter of the future first khalif,
Abū Bakr, when she was six, although the marriage was not consummated
until she was nine.

social, economic, familial, and matrimonial natures, as well as deal with relations with slaves, Jews, and Christians. Every time a problem was submitted to him, Muhammad responded, sometimes only after several days, with an answer in the form of a revelation. In this sense the answer was presented as the outcome of a "descent" of God over him.

Qur'ānic revelations are, in fact, fundamental dogma for Muslims. In Christian revelation, the writer of the sacred text is considered a coauthor with God, and the word is produced under the influence of the Holy Spirit. Christians speak of the Bible as the product of divine "inspiration". When a Christian opens the Gospel, he reads: the Gospel of Jesus Christ *according to* Matthew, Mark, Luke, or John. This "according to" is essential, and the style of one or another evangelist is clearly recognizable. In Islam, this is not the case: the Qur'ān is not considered a mere revealed text from Allah but rather *munzal* (descended)[16] upon Muhammad. The text is simply the literal transcription of an "uncreated" Qur'ān, which has always been with God and has "descended" in the form of a historical Qur'ān.

Based on some verses, the Muslim tradition suggests that this "descent" happened at the moment of Muhammad's prophetic call on the Night of Destiny. The Qur'ān says: "We revealed this on the Night of Qadr. Would that you knew what the night of Qadr is like! Better is the Night of Qadr than a thousand months. On that night the angels and the Spirit by their Lord's leave come down with each decree. That night is peace, till break of dawn." [17] Another

---

[16] *Munzal* comes from the Arabic verb *anzala* (to send down), which is usually translated "to reveal".

[17] The entire sura 97, the Night of al-Qadr. In the Penguin Classics edition, the word *Qadr* is asserted to mean literally "glory"; this is, in fact, an interpretation, for the word does not literally mean "glory" but also means "power", "honor", and/or "destiny".

reference is found in the first verses of sura (chapter) 44, Smoke: "*Ḥā'* and *mīm*.[18] By the Glorious Book, We revealed it on a blessed night to give warning."

Muslims believe that during that night, the Qur'ān, which up to that moment stayed in heaven "inscribed on a *guarded tablet*" (emphasis ours),[19] was literally "sent down" upon Muhammad, who later communicated it, "in pieces", to his followers, according to circumstances. Hence, it is not Muhammad's creation: he is simply the material "retransmitter" of a text "dictated" to him by God through the Archangel Gabriel.

Allow me a personal memory: at an oral graduation exam that I once took in Cairo, I was asked the question "Who is the author of the Qur'ān?" Obviously, as a Christian, I could not answer "God" to this trick question, but I knew that if I did not, I would risk failing the exam. Behind me, a Muslim friend kept telling me: "Say it is God and get it over with!" God inspired me with a good answer: "For Muslims, it is God." It was a descriptive but not a normative answer!

9.   *What is the theological consequence of the dogma that the Qur'ān is considered "the tongue of God"?*

If the Qur'ān was indeed "sent down" by Allah, there is no possibility of a critical or historical interpretation, not even for those aspects that are evidently related to the customs of a particular historical period and culture. In the Christian context, biblical criticism, which some wrongly assert did not develop until the Age of Enlightenment, was already

[18] The letters of the Arabic alphabet that correspond to *ḥ* and *m*. Their function at the beginning of the verse is not clear.

[19] Al-Burūj, sura 85:22. The Penguin Classics edition interprets the verse to mean "inscribed on an imperishable tablet".

in place from the time of the Fathers of the Church. They reasoned that if the biblical text is revealed by God through human manners, this means that the word of God is also received according to the contingent conditions in which the audience lived.

In the history of Islam, at a certain point, it was decided that it was no longer possible to interpret the text. Hence, today, even the mere attempt to understand its meaning and what message it aims to communicate in a certain context is regarded as a desire to challenge it. And this is a true tragedy for the Islamic world: it is not clear who decided it, but everybody accepts this postulate. Since the eleventh century, the "door of interpretation"[20] has been considered closed to individuals, and nobody can open it any longer. The great scholar al-Ghazālī[21] is probably the last Muslim who legally rethought Islam in a definitive way.

In the course of history, many reformers arose on the scene, but they were unable to impose themselves or their ideas on the whole Muslim community. With regard to the role of reason in interpreting the Qur'ān, Averroes[22] wrote a famous work titled *On the Harmony between Reason and the Revealed Law*. In it, he argued that man has the *right* to interpret (*ta'wīl*) the Qur'ān. Indeed, man has the *duty* to interpret it, not just to comment (*tafsīr*) on it, in order to grasp its authentic meaning, in reference to the times in which he is living.

In modern times as well, many efforts have been made in this direction but almost always in vain. The weight of

[20] In Arabic, *bāb al-ijtihād*.

[21] Abū Ḥāmid Muḥammad al-Ghazālī (1058–1111), also called Algazel; a Muslim theologian, thinker, and author of many treatises on philosophy and doctrine.

[22] Abū al-Wālīd Muḥammad ibn Rushd, an Arab philosopher born in Córdoba in 1126.

the tradition and, above all, the fear of questioning the acquired security of the text have created a taboo: the Qur'ān cannot be interpreted, nor can it be critically rethought.

10.   *When were all the revelations [to Muhammad] collected into a single book?*

Two decades after Muhammad's death, the revelations were collected into a book. He never wanted this collection to be assembled during his lifetime. Therefore, the suras were memorized and, sometimes, copied onto pottery fragments, inscribed on palm leaves or parchment, and even marked onto camel bones. The khalif 'Uthmān[23] ordered that all these various fragments be collected with the purpose of creating a *mus-ḥaf*, a book. In fact, 'Uthmān wished to confront definitively the problem caused by the diffusion of many different versions of the Qur'ān. He gathered the seven most famous *ḥuffāz* (memorizers), who had learned by heart some passages of the Qur'ān, and created an official version called *'uthmana.*

Despite his efforts, other problems persisted for a long time. During that period, the Arabs did not use dots with the letters of the alphabet, and this could cause a mix-up among different letters written in identical shape. In fact, it is dots that indicate—according to their number and position under or over the letter—the difference between certain letters, such as *b*, *t*, *th*, *n*, and *y*; thus their omission could produce a wrong reading of the text. Moreover, the vocalic signs, fundamental in a Semitic language in order to read correctly the short vowels, were missing. In sura 30, for instance, it is not clear whether one should read *ghalaba*

---

[23] 'Uthmān ibn 'Affān, first among the prominent nobles of Mecca to convert to Islam. In 644 he succeeded 'Umar as third khalif. He was assassinated in 656.

al-Rūm or *ghuliba al-Rūm*: "the Romans won" or "the Romans have been defeated".[24] It is not a small difference.

Once the official version was published and disseminated, the khalif 'Uthmān ordered the destruction of all other versions. Hence, the *'uthmana* version realized on the khalif's initiative is the Qur'ān we have today. It is the result of compromises between the seven *huffāz*, who often differed one from the other. Therefore, it is impossible to assert with any degree of certainty that a particular section of the Qur'ān is the authentic statement truly pronounced by Muhammad. The original revelations were made over a period of eight thousand days between the years 610 and 632, and no human being could pretend to have such a perfect memory to recall, after many years, the exact words heard only once.

When the Fathers of the Church wrote in Greek, they did not quote the Gospels literally. Such a thing (not quoting literally) would have been considered a grave offense against the Qur'ān. I remember participating in a meeting on Muslim-Christian dialogue in Rome during which I witnessed an embarrassing situation for a Jordanian *imām* who was requested to say a prayer. While reciting from memory some verses of the Qur'ān, the poor man made a mistake, and immediately the Muslims in the audience started to grumble and then corrected him. He tried to continue on but then made a second and a third mistake, and finally stopped and went away very upset and full of shame. He had, in fact, scandalized Muslims in the audience by deforming the uncreated word of God.

For Muslims, the Qur'ān can be compared to Christ: Christ is the Word of God made flesh, while the Qur'ān— please forgive my play on words—is the word "made paper",

---

[24] In Arabic, the term *Rūm*, which means Romans, indicates the Byzantines of the eastern Roman Empire.

fixed on paper. This comparison should allow Muslims to consider the Qur'ān as both *divine* and *human* at the same time, just as Christians acknowledge Jesus' two natures. However, Muslims consider the Qur'ān as only divine.

11.   *Are the 114 chapters, or suras, that form the Qur'ān chronologically ordered according to the times of their revelation?*

Apart from the first sura, the one called *fātiḥa*—that is, "the opening sura"—all the others are ordered according to their length, from the longest to the shortest. There exists, however, an approximate chronological classification of the different chapters. When one opens a copy of the Qur'ān in Arabic, one finds under each sura's title a notation indicating that "this sura descended after this other." One ought not to think that a single sura corresponds to a single intervention or comment by Muhammad. Many suras, in fact, contain verses that "descended" in different moments.

12.   *For those individuals who know how to read Arabic, does the Qur'ān objectively offer something surprising and extraordinary?*

Many passages have an exceptional force of attraction, while others are a bit strange-sounding and have an enigmatic message. Some portions completely escape comprehension but arouse marvel as dazzling syntactical constructions that have a magical effect. If I were to write in this style today, it would be considered abnormal and artificial. Besides these kinds of verses, there exist others that are very boring and devoid of all poetic effect. Many of these verses are legislative texts that do not seem to have any poetic or spiritual inspiration.

For a person from a Christian culture, the reading of the Qur'ān is a bizarre experience and, after a while, a disappointing one as well. A reader immediately discovers that

the Qur'ān offers nothing comparable to the Bible. There
exist some passages that recall the Bible, and these are surely
among the most beautiful in the Qur'ān, but there are also
pages and pages of practical directions about matters concerning daily life. Alongside a reading about Muhammad's
personal problems with his wives, one can find beautiful
spiritual reflections and prayers.

One of the most beautiful chapters is number 112, the
"sura of the pure faith", which proclaims: "Say: 'God is
One, the Eternal God. He begot none, nor was He begotten. None is equal to Him'". The statement "He begot
none, nor was He begotten" was originally addressed to
pagan Arabs, but it soon became understood as addressed
to Christians. It contradicted their creedal statement that
declares Jesus Christ is "begotten, not made". Today, when
pronouncing these verses, no Muslim thinks of pagans, but
he thinks of Christians. Other suras are quite boring. Even
those who read the Qur'ān in Arabic do not perceive what
Muslims call *i'jāz al-Qur'ān*, that is, the "miracle of the
Qur'ān".

13.   *In saying the "miracle of the Qur'ān", are you referring
to the belief that the Qur'ān descended from heaven as it is?*

Not exactly! For Muslims, the *i'jāz* (miracle) is the inimitable literary style of the Qur'ān. At a certain point, people
asked Muhammad: "As you claim to be a prophet, which
sign do you give us? Do a miracle! You talk about Moses'
miracles and those of Jesus: and your miracles, where are
they?" And he answers: "My miracle is the Qur'ān: produce one similar verse." The Muslim tradition says that
the Bedouins were not able to produce a single verse that
could be compared to the beauty of the Qur'ān, and they
define this as Muhammad's doing a "miracle". Muhammad,

in reality, did not perform any miracles, even if the late tradition ascribes many to him, in imitation of the prophets.

Muslims claim that, by comparing Muhammad's sayings—collected in the *ḥadīth*—with the Qur'ān through a syntactical and lexical computer analysis, they can demonstrate that there is nothing in common between the two texts, because the Qur'ān is the language of God while the *ḥadīth* is the language of Muhammad. But this statement is without foundation because such a study has never been done, and a philological examination shows the real influence of events in Muhammad's life on the qur'ānic text. For example, some Ethiopian words[25] that were typically Christian appear in the text only in the period following the emigration of Muslims to Ethiopia.

14.   *Muslims commonly claim that Muhammad was illiterate. From this fact and from the text of the Qur'ān, could not we deduce that something "miraculous" took place?*

Western scholars and many Muslim scholars deny that Muhammad was illiterate. When the Qur'ān mentions the word *ummī* (illiterate), it is opposed to the word that indicates those who have a sacred text. The *ummiyyūn* (plural of *ummī*) are not those people who cannot read but are those who do not possess a sacred book. The statement that "Muhammad is the prophet of the *ummiyyūn*" should be interpreted in the sense that Muhammad considered himself a prophet to pagans, not to Jews and Christians, who already had a sacred text. The meaning of *ummiyyūn* is similar to the Latin *gentes*, peoples. *Ummī* was used to describe Saint Paul as the apostle of the Gentiles, or pagans. It is likely that this same meaning has been adopted by the Jews,

[25] Like *zabūr* (psalter) or *ḥawārī* (apostle of Jesus).

who use a similar expression—*goyim*—to indicate the other nations.

C. The Five Pillars of Islam

15.   *What are the basic fundamentals of the Islamic faith?*

Islam bases itself on five pillars: the profession of faith in Allah and in his prophet (*shahāda*); the ritual prayer five times a day (*ṣalāt*); the offering of the ritual charity, that is, almsgiving (*zakāt*); the fasting in the month of Ramaḍān (*ṣawm*); and finally, the pilgrimage to Mecca (*ḥajj*), to be accomplished at least once in a lifetime for those who have the financial means.

It is difficult to make a comparison of these five pillars with the Christian commandments. For example, prayer for a Christian is a way of addressing God, which can have different forms, including a liturgical one. In Islam, the perspective is mainly juridical. For a Muslim, the ritual prayer[26] is performed by accomplishing certain rites, such as prostration, in a formally perfect way. It is true that the *ṣalāt* lasts from five to ten minutes and is performed five times a day, but it is a rite. Those who fulfill it in a formally correct way, in conformity with the prescribed rite, after having purified themselves with the ablutions, have prayed; he who prays without observing the purification ritual is as if he had not prayed.

For example, when a woman has her menstrual period, she is considered impure; thus she cannot accomplish the ritual prayer, and therefore she must make this prayer time up on another day. The same is true for fasting: on some

---

[26] The nonritual prayer, which most resembles the Christian one, is called *duʿāʾ*.

days during Ramaḍān, women normally cannot fast because they are impure, and they must therefore make up for the days lost in Ramaḍān during the rest of the year. It is an objective matter, not a subjective one.

Let us use the example of fasting again: it consists in abstaining from eating, drinking, smoking, or introducing anything into the body from dawn to sunset, but after sunset one can eat more and better than on normal days. This practice is not the original ascetic spirit of Ramaḍān; rather, it is a human accommodation that has lasted for many years. As early as the eleventh century, al-Ghazālī strongly condemned this betrayal of the original spirit of Ramaḍān. Yet those individuals who formally respect the ritual precepts have actually fasted. Islam, then, is a normative religion, and this is both its strength and its weakness.

Moreover, a fundamental aspect of prayer and fasting is that these are collective actions. Worshippers all gather together, at the same time, to complete the same gestures and to pronounce the same prayers. The same thing happens with the pilgrimage to Mecca. It is an extraordinary meeting that involves millions of people. This collective synchronism gives immense strength to Muslims and underlines their unity. Ramaḍān, as well, offers similar suggestions: all Muslims fast during the day; then, after sunset, they all rush to the water, to drink. It is a social event of great importance that sometimes involves non-Muslim citizens as well. This is the force of Islam, the religious vision wisely wished by Muhammad.

16.   *Do you mean to say that other religions are more difficult to practice or are more "demanding" of their faithful?*

Muslims claim that Judaism is an "earthly" religion (which is not true) and that Christianity is heavenly and sublime but so idealistic that nobody is able to live it fully. Islam combined these earthly and heavenly elements into a religion of moderation and reason.

In reality, many teachings of Islam are not rational at all, but by dint of repeating them for centuries, they are accepted. Take, for instance, the claim that the Qur'ān descended from heaven or that Muhammad is the prophet of God. Neither claim can be proven, nor can either claim be admitted to by reason without the support of faith. Therefore, those non-Muslims who lack this faith hardly recognize the prophetic character of Muhammad.

Islam is more demanding in certain things and less demanding in others. On the one hand, it is a demanding faith because it imposes prayer five times a day and fasting from dawn to sunset for a month. On the other hand, it is a lenient religion because there is no need for many questions about individual requirements because everyone does the prescribed activity at the same time. Doing something with others is a much simpler way of proceeding. Islam is relatively easy to practice in Muslim countries because there is a very strong social support system that surrounds a Muslim, but it is more difficult in non-Muslim countries. To be precise, for immigrants, because there is no longer the social support system or communal pressure to conform, the practice of religion must be the result of a totally personal choice.

Islam is more of a communal than an individual religion. The Muslim is not lost in complicated considerations about knowing what to do or what not to do. A Muslim often has predetermined answers and thus fewer problems of conscience than Christians. When confronting problems of conscience, the answer for a Christian is not simply dictated by the Church but is determined by his free use of reason and adherence to what the Church teaches. However, the modern world poses many questions for contemporary Muslims that were not foreseen at the beginning, which leaves them in doubt. This is why many Muslims turn to the *fuqahā'* (plural of *faqīh*), the jurist consultants, to obtain valid answers to their new moral questions.

17. *Is there no Muslim spirituality, then? It almost seems as if Muslims have no spiritual requirements or needs.*

I do not wish to absolutely deny the existence of a Muslim spirituality. On the contrary, their spirituality can be very deep, as in the case of mystics (*sūfī*), but Muslim religiosity can also be very superficial due to the fact that many requirements are satisfied by simply observing external prescriptions. In Christianity, the spiritual life of the individual believer is a central element, while in Islam this is less common. The legalism of Islam recalls that of Judaism.

It is not by chance that the main science of Islam is jurisprudence, not theology or spirituality, as in the Christian tradition. In Islam the scholar (or the *faqīh*, singular of *fuqahā'*) is the one who knows all jurisprudence. The faithful turn to him to ask whether, in certain situations, they can, for example, do their prayers, and he indicates what they must do to pray validly. Open any book of Muslim tradition, of jurisprudence, or of *hadīth*, and you will find everything, starting with the rules of purification, that is normative for the ablutions necessary for prayer or fasting. Even the text that collects Ayatollah Khomeini's sayings, for example, lists a series of directives regarding purity, prayer, and fasting, all conceived as rituals.

Purification is a juridical act, not a spiritual one. The *fuqahā'* remind us of the "doctors of the law" in the Gospels. Muslim purification is conceived in the same manner as in the Old Testament, of which we have an echo in the debate between Jesus and the Pharisees, the recognized specialists on the Torah: it is exclusively an exterior purity. Against this conception, Christ reacted by saying: "Do you not see that whatever goes into the mouth passes into the stomach, and so passes on? But what comes out of the mouth proceeds from the heart, and this defiles a man." [27]

This vision of the Old Testament can also be found in Islam: if someone does not do the prescribed ablutions, his prayer is not accepted by God. The rules of purity forbid a man to touch a woman because she could be having her menstrual period, which makes her impure, and by touching her, that man would become impure as well.

Everything is calculated but framed in the context of the Arab cultural world of the seventh century. For this reason, if one tries to understand Muhammad's project for the Muslim religion, what emerges is an all-inclusive design for a social, political, cultural, and religious community.

To be a Muslim means, for many believers, to pray or to dress in a certain way; to eat some foods and refuse others (especially pork and blood meats); and to behave in a specifically prescribed way, both externally and internally. In this regard, one must note a radical difference with Christianity, which is not a religion in the sense that it is not a human attempt to represent the Mystery with a certain idea of God and to put into practice a series of ethical norms by requiring adherents to behave in a coherent way; rather, Christianity is an Event, the Event of the revelation of God, by which he answers a human longing and makes himself present to man by taking man's condition upon himself.

[27] Mt 15:17–18.

II. Can Islam Change?

A. Unity and Plurality

18. *One often hears that it is wrong to conceive of Islam as a monolithic block with a single religious, cultural, and anthropological profile. Today many scholars insist on an interpretation of Islam based on its plurality that avoids generalizations and a superficial reading of its complex reality. Do you agree with this perspective?*

Theologically, the unity of the Muslim community is based on the oneness of God and on Muhammad's prophecy summarized in the first pillar: God is absolutely one (*tawḥīd*); Muhammad is his last messenger and the seal of the prophets (*khātam al-nabiyyīn*), that is, the one who transmits to mankind the last message of God and corrects and fulfills all the preceding revelations, bringing them to their completion.

Practically, the unity of the Muslim community realizes itself in the other four pillars: ritual prayer, charity, fasting, and the pilgrimage. The evocative force of the five pillars and their effectiveness in strengthening unity among the faithful are nurtured by the unanimity and simplicity of gestures and words, rituals, times, and movements (e.g., kneeling in the direction of Mecca during the prayer, walking around the Kaʿba, etc.). In these actions and words lies Muhammad's genius in creating and proposing simple but strongly unifying rites.

The global Muslim community has the Qur'ān as its common reference, and the text is recited only in Arabic (even by those who do not know this language), in a uniform manner and with no variation.[1] This text is considered the divine word communicated by God to his last messenger, Muhammad, from the uncreated copy that is in heaven with God.

During the centuries in which Islam spread into diverse areas of the world, it is undeniable that for a long time plurality existed in Islam's expression at the sociocultural level. African Islam, for example, is normally less closed and dogmatic, as evidenced by the coexistence of Christians, Muslims, and pagans in the same family or by the propagation of ascetical offshoots, such as Sufism and the brotherhoods, which would be condemned or hardly tolerated elsewhere. It should be noted that Lebanese Islam is more open to modernity. This is fairly typical of any religion that has expanded into many different parts of the world. However, the phenomenon does not alter the fact that Islam, beyond its sociological versions, has strong common origins on the dogmatic and ritual level and is considered by Muslims as a global project that is at the same time religious, cultural, social, and political. It is a mentality inherited after centuries of historical development and cemented today by the hegemony of the richest Islamic countries, especially Saudi Arabia. Through financial support, the Saudis influence the ideas and behaviors of millions of Muslim faithful and contribute to a process of unification of thought.

By way of example, Egypt is the Arab country with the highest number of Muslims and up to now has produced

---

[1] In some countries, the habit of reading the Qur'ān in the local language or in the languages of the different communities that attend the mosque is spreading. But this custom does not cancel the fundamental rule that imposes its recitation (talāwa) in Arabic.

the majority of films in Arabic. About ten years ago, the Saudis acquired control over Egyptian film distribution and established some strict rules for the circulation of films. These regulations require that films must meet specific standards— for example, women must wear a veil, there must be a reference to prayer by illustrating the faithful who kneel to pray or someone who closes his shop to go to the mosque, and they must not show alcoholic beverages on screen.

Also in Egypt, Saudi Arabia financed the creation of hundreds of village "Azharic"[2] schools (small Islamic elementary and middle schools that teach strong Islamic beliefs that imprint traditionalist Wahhabism[3] on their students), which are officially recognized by the government. These schools contribute to the creation of a mentality derived from the most intransigent orthodoxy, the same orthodoxy that nourishes the fundamentalist and radical groups, especially among the younger generation. It is precisely in this mentality that one finds the nurturing, the cultural soil, and sometimes even the followers of the main protagonists who undertake violent actions in the name of Islam.

B. Religious Authority and the Problem of Representation

19.   *It is said that Islam does not know any category of authority or of religious hierarchy; nonetheless, some individuals are*

[2] Al-Azhar University was founded by the Fatimite in 973, four years after their arrival in Egypt, as a Shiite theological mosque-school. The name al-Azhar means "the Resplendent", an allusion to Fatima al-Zahrā', Muhammad's daughter and ʿAlīʾs wife, whose name was given to the dynasty. The university is attended by students from all over the Islamic world, and it had an important role in the history of Islamic Sunni thought.

[3] In reference to the strict interpretation of Islam formulated by the theologian Muhammad bin ʿAbdil-Wahhāb (1703–1787). Wahhabism is prevalent in Saudi Arabia.

recognized as authoritative. What is the degree of authority of the muftī, *sheikh,* imām, *and* ayatollah?

The statement that "there is no clergy in Islam" is a wide-spread error in the Western world. If by "clergy" one means what Catholics or Orthodox Christians mean, then it is true: Islam has neither patriarchs nor cardinals, neither bishops nor priests. But if one means that there is neither an authority nor a hierarchy in Islam, the statement is false. In a certain sense, clericalism in Islam is even stronger than it is in the Catholic Church.

Allow me to explain. All Muslims are equal, but many dedicate themselves to the study of Islam in its various articulations. One who studies the tradition, the *ḥadīth*, becomes a *muḥaddith*; he who studies the law becomes a *faqīh*, or *mufassir* (doctor of the law); he who makes general studies of the Qur'ān and tradition becomes an *imām*, who leads the prayer at the mosque; he who has a beautiful voice and dedicates himself, with an economic compensation, to sing the call to prayer five times a day is called a *muezzin*; and he who enjoys a recognized religious authority is the sheikh, meaning "old man" but also "presbyter" in Arabic and in many other languages. These are categories described with Arabic terms.

In Persian, we find other terms used to describe the same positions, such as *mullah*, *sayyed*, *ḥojjatoleslām*, and *āyatollāh*. In the Shiite world, the hierarchy is more structured, according to the degree of knowledge acquired by the faithful and the number of texts studied, which can amount to thousands. In short, it is a classification with titles that correspond to different levels of learning. The Shiites also promote discipleship—that is, every devout person has a guide, chosen from among the *A'īmah* (plural of *imām*), to whom he pays the so-called *khums*, a fifth of his profits, and with whom he establishes a strict master-disciple relationship.

The hierarchy is less evident in the Sunni world, but it is equally present. If one considers Egypt, a 90 percent Sunni country, one notices the strong authority an *imām* or a sheikh exercises over the faithful. This is certainly related to the leader's level of education. The more a person is educated, the less he feels dependent. But because the majority of Muslims do not have the possibility of deepening their knowledge about the doctrine and legal aspects of Islam, it is easier for them to submit to the judgments of the sheikhs.

There are also the "supreme authorities", such as the Islamic school al-Azhar University in Cairo. The school is an ancient institution with wide renown in the Sunni world. It plays the role of arbiter of modern Islamic thought. In fact, the moral authority of the rector of al-Azhar goes beyond Egyptian borders, even if it does not correspond with that of the pope in Catholicism.

Every Muslim country has its own grand *muftī*, a word deriving from *fatwā*, which is a jurisprudential pronouncement. Traditionally appointed by the government, the *muftī* is the one who issues *fatwā*, sometimes suggested by the government itself. People with this charge receive salaries from the government, even in Lebanon, a multidenominational country. It is interesting to observe that the Lebanese government proposed paying a salary even to Christian religious leaders, but they refused in order to remain independent from political authorities. In contrast, all Muslim sheikhs accept the government payment, which implies that if someone is not appreciated by the government because of his overly independent thinking, he can be dismissed and replaced.

Having said this, it must be stated again that there is no juridical authority similar to that of the bishops or the pope in the Roman Catholic Church, because the authority of

Muslim religious leaders is only a moral one. Their opinions are respected, but they are not binding on anyone; and this is quite different from the way authority is conceived in Catholic and Orthodox Christianity and, to a lesser but still significant degree, in Protestant churches.

20. *Are recent problems a result of the end of the khalifate, which represented, at least formally, the unity of the Islamic world?*

During the first centuries of Islam, the khalif made decisions on religious matters after consulting with jurists. The abolition of the khalifate in 1924 highlighted even more the weakness that the Islamic world already experienced, and the abolition resulted in the growth of groups and local authorities that make autonomous decisions.

Muslims tried for some time to fill this void by proposing a new khalif: King Fu'ād[4] of Egypt or King 'Abdul-'Azīz[5] of Arabia. When this new arrangement did not work, the Muslims realized that nobody possessed widely recognized authority and that Islam was no longer a strong and united world. There was an attempt to compensate for this void with the creation of international Muslim organizations, but these have only an advisory and not a juridical authority.

Today, Islam presents itself as a fragmented religion, and this causes many problems when an "official" representative is needed in order to solve serious problems and answer difficult questions. It suffices to think about the recent controversy raised by the appeals of Bin Lādin or other

[4] King of Egypt from 1923 to 1936. Before that date, he governed with the title of sultan.

[5] Founder of the kingdom of Saudi Arabia in 1932 and father of all the following Saudi sovereigns.

Muslim leaders in order to summon the masses to rise up "in the name of Islam". These appeals were disavowed by other Muslim leaders or organizations, also "in the name of Islam".

In forming public opinion, one of the most paradoxical aspects of the international crisis that followed the attacks on the World Trade Center "Twin Towers" buildings in New York City was the number of contradictory declarations made with quotations from the Qur'ān and from Islamic tradition, which dramatically confirmed the absence of any authoritative position that was unanimously recognized by Muslims at the international level.

21.   *Is dealing with a series of Muslim representatives who hold contradictory opinions inevitable, then?*

Unfortunately, the answer is yes. The most evident case was the long opposing "war of *fatwā*" between the *muftī* of Egypt and the rector of al-Azhar. The disputes concerned religious matters, such as whether the charging of bank interest or the practice of infibulation (the surgical practice of closing the vagina with stitches) should be considered licit, or whether Palestinian suicide bombers should be considered martyrs, or whether abortion should be permitted in some cases.

The point is that in Islam, *sharīʿa* (Islamic law) is based on a copious number of very hard-to-memorize *Aḥādīth* (sayings of Muhammad). For this reason, the *fuqahā'* (the doctors of the law) often have an almost absolute authority over the faithful. The situation reminds us of the Gospels, with the doctors of the law and the Pharisees, on whom the Jews felt totally dependent for distinguishing between true and false, licit and illicit.

Complicating matters even further, a closing of the "door of interpretation" in Islam came in the eleventh century, as we already mentioned.[6] The "closure" was a silent agreement among leaders that everything that was in need of clarification about Islam had already been explained by the great masters of the juridical schools.[7] This *ijmā* (consensus) in practice prevented Islam from renewing itself to deal with the challenges of the modern world.

Today, liberal Muslims question whether the Islamic juridical system agreed upon ten centuries ago is still able to definitively solve the problems confronting Muslims in the twenty-first century. Many new questions have arisen since then, but no one is able to look for answers that differ from those that were developed by the time the door of interpretation was closed. Obviously the great theologians did not make any pronouncement on the use of cars or television; therefore, the principle of *qiyās* (analogy) is used today in order to make an analogical transposition of a similar issue from the ancient tradition to answer modern questions. Clearly the "answer" often consists of intellectual acrobatics that have nothing to do either with real life or with the spirit of jurisprudence.

Often completely different motives are behind certain judgments. For instance, the fact that in Saudi Arabia women are prohibited from driving is directly connected to the male's desire to control the female. Saudi women can ride in a car but only with a driver who takes her where she wants, waits for her, and then reports to her husband where she went, what she did, and whom she met.

---

[6] See question 9, p. 43 above.

[7] The Sunni schools are four: the Ḥanafi, the Shāfiʿi, the Māliki, and the Ḥanbali. The Shiite school is called Jaʿfari. See also the Glossary of terms below.

C. *Jihād*: A Holy War or a Spiritual Struggle?

22.   *What is the meaning of the very common but often misunderstood word* jihād*?*

The word *jihād* derives from the root *j-h-d*, which in Arabic means an effort, normally the effort related to war. In the Qur'ān, the word *jihād* is always used to mean "fight for God", according to the complete expression *jihād fī sabīl Allāh* (fight for the way to God); therefore, it is translated into the European languages by Muslims as "holy war".

This translation was recently called into question by some scholars, especially in the West, who consider *jihād* not as war but as a spiritual struggle, an inner effort. A distinction is made between *jihād akbar* and *jihād asghar*, the great *jihād* and the small *jihād*. The former is the struggle against self-ishness and the evils of society. It is an ethical and spiritual effort. The small *jihād* is the holy war that must be fought against the infidels in the name of God.

This is an elaboration that corresponds neither to the Islamic tradition nor to modern language. All the Islamist groups who adopt the word *jihād* into their organization name do not intend it be understood in its mystical meaning but rather with its violent connotation. As a result, the many books published in the last years on *jihād* all refer to holy war. Therefore, on the sociohistorical level, from the Qur'ān onward, the ordinary meaning of *jihād* is unequivocal. The term *jihād* indicates the Muslim war in the name of God to defend Islam.

Let me explain. The *jihād* is an obligation for all adult Muslims, in particular for males. Islam, in fact, knows two kinds of obligations: the individual obligation and the collective obligation. The *jihād* is a collective obligation in the sense that the whole community is bound to participate if it feels endangered. Only the *imām* has the right or duty to proclaim *jihād*; but once he does so, all adult male Muslims must enroll.

This is an obligation established for the Muslim in the Qur'ān, which often rebukes the "lukewarm" for not participating in war but remaining quietly and calmly in the safety of their homes and calls them "hypocrites". This obligation was invoked by Muhammad at the beginning, and it concerns both defensive war—that is, when Islam is attacked—and preventive war, when the risk of being attacked is imminent. *Jihād* must be fought until the last enemy has gone or has been killed.

23.   *Are there precise rules for proclaiming the* jihād*? And how do you explain the fact that sometimes—for example, in the Iran-Iraq War, the Gulf War, or any of the historical wars between different Arab-Muslim dynasties—Muslim countries fight against other Muslim countries?*

A war between brothers in the faith is illicit and inconceivable in Islamic juridical terms. For this reason, if a Muslim leader wants to make war on a Muslim country, he first has to declare the opposing country an unbeliever, an atheist—in Arabic, *kāfir*. By declaring the other nation *kāfir*, the declaration of war becomes legitimate and the conflict unavoidable because it is conducted against unbelievers.

Before declaring war on his enemies, Muhammad invited them to convert to Islam, repeating the invitation three times. If they refused, he informed them that an attack was imminent, and if they still persisted in refusing to convert, he attacked them. This process may seem like something that belongs to the past, but in reality we can observe its practice in the Iran-Iraq conflict (which resulted in one million casualties) or in the Gulf War. Each faction in the conflicts declared the enemy *kāfir*, proclaimed itself a champion of Islam, and put Islamic symbols on its flag. Iraq, a country that considered itself a secular state, added the words *Allāh-u Akbar* (God is the greatest) to its national flag, which evidenced a religious reason to attack the enemy "in the name of God".

The same can be said for the conflicts in Kosovo, Chechnya, Afghanistan, the Philippines, the Moluccas, or wherever Muslims are at war. In these places, we see armed groups arriving from different countries to fight *jihād* against the enemies of Islam (who are often Christians). The foreign fighters call themselves *mujāhidīn* (which, etymologically, means those who make the *jihād*) and operate in different countries to foster revolutions or to support rebels and national liberation movements.[8]

Here it becomes clear that the goal of fighting for Islam at an international level prevails over political-national motivations. For the *mujāhidīn* groups, the concept of Islamic community (*umma*) supersedes that of individual citizenship (*waṭan*). A confirmation of this attitude has come in the recent conflict in Afghanistan. Many Muslims, living in Arab as well as Western countries, voluntarily enlisted and chose to fight alongside the Taliban forces with the clear purpose of defending Islam threatened by the "infidels".

It is interesting to note that even in Palestine, where the conflict is primarily a struggle for the national independence of Palestine from Israeli occupation, instead of keeping the debate focused on the political field of national claims, the Islamic countries continue to transform it into a war of religions, into a *jihād* for the liberation of that land. The

---

[8] For further information on the different Islamic radical movements in the world, see Camille Eid, *Osama e i suoi fratelli* [Osama and His Brothers] (Milan: Pimedit, 2001).

fundamental problem causing conflict is a political one; however, many fanatical Palestinians and Israelis insist religion is the root cause. In fact, orthodox Jews, as well as orthodox Muslims, hold a nearly identical idea of religion and state. It is a concept where everything is intertwined and where the different spheres lose their autonomy.

24. *In the Western world and in some moderate Muslim environments, people often say that the* mujāhidīn *are not true Muslims, that their actions are contrary to the spirit of Islam, that Islam etymologically means "peace" and "tolerance", and so on. Is this opinion correct?*

Most Westerners who accept these statements usually know very little about Islam. So they willingly accept these erroneous theories coming from Muslim sources.

The words *islām* and *salām* actually derive from the same root, but they do not have a direct relationship. In Arabic, the root *s-l-m*, equivalent to *sh-l-m* in Jewish and in all Semitic languages, means "to be healthy", "to be in peace"; and there is a semantic relationship between peace, salvation, and health. In Arabic, *salām* means "peace", *salāma* means "health", and *islām* means "submission" or "surrender". The word *islām* derives from the verb *aslama*, which means "to submit" or "to abandon oneself to"; therefore, *islām* is the act of abandoning oneself, or of submitting oneself, to God. It does not mean "to put oneself in a state of peace", even if someone, for spiritual reasons, might offer this nonetymological meaning.

Violence was clearly part of Muhammad's life, as we already pointed out in chapter 1. Here it is interesting to note that the first biographies of the founder are not named *sīra*, as they came to be called in the third century of Hegira (the ninth century of the Christian era), but *kitāb al-maghāzī*, that is, the "Book of the Raids". It was Muhammad himself, as a political leader, who systematically conducted these raids. He organized them and then conquered, one after the other, the different Arab tribes. When the tribes submitted to him and to his God, they paid a tribute, which allowed Muhammad to start new conquests.

Following Muhammad's death (632), many tribes revolted against his successor, khalif Abū Bakr al-Ṣiddīq (632–634). The revolt began when the tribal leaders refused to continue paying the tribute, so the khalif declared war on them. Muslim historiographers call these wars *ḥurūb al-ridda* (the wars of the apostates). From the conflict came the obligation to kill whoever drew back, the apostate who denies his faith.[9] It must be remembered that the supporters of the khalif had informed him simply that the tribes refused to pay tribute, not that they rejected Islam. In reality, the tribes considered Muhammad as more a political leader than a religious prophet, and so at his death they did not want to recognize another leader.

Violence was definitely a part of the rapid rise and expansion of Islam. At the time, no one found anything blameworthy in Muhammad's military actions since wars were part of the Arab Bedouin culture. Today, the problem is that the fiercest Muslim groups keep adopting that model. They say, "We have to take Islam to non-Muslims as the Prophet did, through war and violence", and they base these statements on some verses from the Qur'ān.

25. *And yet the Qur'ān states that there must be no constraint in matters of faith.*

In the Qur'ān, there exist verses in favor of religious tolerance, and other verses that are openly opposed to

[9] See questions 58–61 on apostasy.

tolerance. Usually, Muslims who live in the West often like quoting the former ones, such as verse 256 of the Cow, sura 2, on the prohibition to oblige people to believe. Bonelli's translation says: "There shall be no compulsion in religion, the right way stands out clear from error",[10] and the one by Peirone reads: "Let there be no compulsion in the matter of religious freedom: the straight way stands out easily from Error." [11]

There is also verse 99 of Jonah, sura 10, which, in the translation by Bonelli, says: "But had it been your God's will, those who are on the earth would all have believed; will you then compel men to believe?" Peirone translates, "If God wanted, all those who are on the earth would believe. But you cannot force people to believe!"

These statements clearly indicate tolerance. However, alongside these verses, there exist more aggressive ones, such as the famous verse 29 of Repentance, sura 9. The translation by Bonelli says: "Fight against those who do not believe in God or in the Last Day, nor consider forbidden what God and his apostles have forbidden, nor acknowledge the religion of truth, that is those who have been given the Book, until they pay the *jizya* [tribute] out of hand, with submission." The phrase "those who have been given the Book" obviously refers to Jews and Christians. In Peirone's translation, one reads: "Fight those who are *kāfirūn* [unbelievers] in God and in the Last Day, who do not declare *harām* [unlawful] what God and the *rasūl* [messenger] have declared *harām*. Fight, among the peoples of the Scripture,

---

[10] Luigi Bonelli, trans. *Il Corano più antico* [The Oldest Qur'ān] (Venice: Marsilio, 1991).

[11] Federico Peirone, trans. *Il Corano* [The Qur'ān] (Milan: Oscar Mondadon, 1987). [Following the Italian edition of this present work, in order to make the same clear comparison between the verses taken from two different Italian translations of the Qur'ān, in this instance I have chosen to translate the Bonelli and Peirone quotations into English instead of using the English translation of the Qur'ān that was used elsewhere in this book. TRANS.]

those who do not practice the true religion. Fight them until they pay, each one their tribute, and only then accept their submission."

See also verse 47 of the Table, sura 5, which says: "Therefore, let those who follow the Gospel judge according to what God has revealed therein. Evildoers are those who do not judge according to God's revelations"; or verse 110 of the 'Imrāns, sura 3, which addresses Muslims, saying: "You are the noblest community ever raised up for mankind. You enjoin justice and forbid evil. You believe in God. Had the People of the Book accepted the Faith, it would surely have been better for them. Some are true believers, but most of them are evildoers." That is to say that the majority of Jews and Christians are evildoers and therefore must be fought as *kuffār* or *kāfirūn*, as unbelievers.

We should not forget that here we are still talking about Christians and Jews and not about polytheists. For polytheists, there is no escape: either they become Muslims or they must be killed. Verse 142 of the same sura asks, "Did you suppose that you would enter Paradise before God has proved the men who fought for Him and endured with fortitude?" while verse 39 of the Spoils, sura 8, recommends: "Make war on them until idolatry shall cease and God's religion shall reign supreme."

Even in the tradition of the *ḥadīth*, ascribed to Muhammad, we find many similar recommendations. In al-Bukhārī's collection,[12] an entire chapter is devoted to *jihād*: here the author deals exclusively with war in God's name. Paragraph 102 of the chapter says, "I received the order of fighting people until they confess there is no other divinity but God.

---

[12] Abū 'Abd Allāh Muḥammad al-Bukhārī (d. 870). He is one of the most noted collectors of *Aḥādīth* traditions; he wrote "*al-Jami' al-Ṣaḥīḥ*", one of the six official *Aḥādīth* collections.

Those who confess it have nothing to fear from me; they cannot be attacked in their person, nor in their own goods, unless in conformity with the right of Islam, and God will be responsible for them." Another *hadīth* ascribes to Muhammad the saying: "Be aware that Paradise is under the shadow of swords."

In the first chapter, paragraph 29, of Ibn Ḥanbal's collection,[13] we find a *hadīth* attributed to Muhammad (I personally doubt its authenticity) in which the prophet of Islam expresses his intention as well as gives an order to his followers to chase Jews and Christians away from the Arabic peninsula until there would be only Muslims left. He stated, "I shall expel Jews and Christians from the Arabs' peninsula, in order to leave only Muslims"; and again, "Expel from the Arabs' peninsula the Jews of the Ḥijāz and the people of Najrān [that is, Christians]".[14] Based on these *hadīth* of questionable attribution, we know that the khalif 'Umar actually chased Christians and Jews away from the Arabic peninsula[15] in the year 20 of Hegira (A.D. 641).

I speak about the violence expressed in the Qur'ān and practiced in Muhammad's life in order to address the idea, widespread in the West, that the violence we see today is a deformation of Islam. We must honestly admit that there

---

[13] Aḥmad b. Ḥanbal al-Shaybani (780–855). He was an important Muslim scholar and the founder of the Ḥanbali school of Islamic jurisprudence. He was also persecuted by the Khalif al-Ma'mūn in 833 because b. Ḥanbal asserted that the Qur'ān is not created.

Ḥanbal did not write himself; it was his disciple, Abu Bakr al-Marwazi, who collected his teachings in twenty volumes called "*al-Jami' al-kabīr*".

[14] The many *hadith* on this matter are collected in André Ferré, "Muhammad a-t-il exclu de l'Arabie les juifs et les chrétiens?" [Did Muhammad Expel Jews and Christians from Arabia?] *Islamochristiana* 16 (1990): 43–65, here 48ff. See also Leone Caetani, *Annali dell'Islam* [Annals of Islam] (Rome: 1920) 5:350–56.

[15] See Ferré, "Muhammad", 48, in particular.

are two readings of the Qur'ān and the *sunna* (Islamic traditions connected to Muhammad): one that opts for the verses that encourage tolerance toward other believers, and one that prefers the verses that encourage conflict. Both readings are legitimate.

Confronted with these contradictory verses, the Muslim tradition was obliged to find a method of interpretation, called "the principle of the abrogating and the abrogated", in Arabic, *al-nāsikh wa-l-mansūkh*. The theory is simple: God, after giving a disposition or an order, can give an opposite order, for contrary reasons. It is then a matter of knowing which one was God's last order, which cancels and abrogates the preceding disposition. The problem was faced by many exegetes, who wrote long treatises titled "On the Abrogating and the Abrogated" without, unfortunately, reaching a consensus that allows a clear statement about what verses have abrogated others. The principle of the abrogating and the abrogated has its foundation in verse 106 of the Cow, sura 2: "If we abrogate a verse or cause it to be forgotten, we will replace it by a better one or one similar. Did you not know that God has power over all things?"

26. *Is this due to the fact that there is no consensus on the exact sequence of the suras?*

Muslim scholars unanimously distinguish the suras of the Mecca period (610–622) from those of the Medina period (622–632). But scholars have not been able to agree on the exact order of internal succession of the suras from these two periods. Rather, the orientalists have tried to distinguish three stages within the Mecca period and, in general, to better specify the internal order of succession by determining some dates.

In Egypt, for example, it is a commonly held opinion that the so-called Verse of the Sword (*āyat al-sayf*) abrogated more than one hundred verses, that is to say, all the "peaceful" ones. The verse reads: "When the sacred months are over slay the idolaters wherever you find them. Arrest them, besiege them, and lie in ambush everywhere for them. If they repent and take to prayer and render the alms levy, allow them to go their way. God is forgiving and merciful" (Repentance 9:5). Today the problem is that, whatever their position, Muslims will not admit that some verses of the Qur'ān no longer have relevance for present situations. Therefore, the *ulemā'* (qur'ānic doctors of the law) are obliged to say that they do not agree with those who choose to adopt the Verse of the Sword as normative, even if they cannot condemn them. Consequently, in the Qur'ān there are two different choices, the aggressive and the peaceful, and both of them are acceptable. There is a need for an authority, unanimously acknowledged by Muslims, that could say: From now on, only this verse is valid. But this does not—and probably will never—happen.

This means that when some fanatics kill children, women, and men in the name of pure and authentic Islam, or in the name of the Qur'ān or of the Muslim tradition, nobody can tell them: "You are not true and authentic Muslims." All they can say is: "Your reading of Islam is not ours." And this is the ambiguity of Islam, from its beginning to the present day: violence is a part of it, although it is also possible to choose tolerance; tolerance is a part of it, but it is also possible to choose violence.

27. *To answer those who raise the question about* jihād, *Muslims state that Christians were worse, implying the Crusades or the colonialist period.*

This is a debate that I would leave to the historians, with the fundamental difference that the Crusaders or the

Christians who fought the war did not pretend to have done it based on the Gospels: instead, they did it in defense of Christianity (or so they thought), or for the defense of their national state, or for the defense of what they considered to be their rights. That is to say, as men belonging to a culture, a nation, a tradition, they went to war. They did not act in the name of the Gospel.

Let us not forget that the Crusades were initially a reaction to the persecutions brought about by the Fatimite khalif al-Ḥākim bi-Amr Allāh (996–1021) against the Christians in Egypt and Syria (which at the time also included the Holy Land). In the year 1008, al-Ḥākim abolished the celebration of Palm Sunday. In 1009, he issued orders "to punish only those [secretaries] who were Christians, having many of them hanged by their hands and deprived of all their possessions".[16] In March 1009, "he sent a letter to Damascus in which he ordered the destruction of the Catholic church consecrated to the Virgin Mary, a big and beautiful church indeed, which was, in fact, pulled down in the month of *rajab* of that same year." [17] On Sunday, August 13, 1009,

> he had the church dedicated to Mary in al-Qanṭarah, in Old Cairo, destroyed. After its complete destruction, he had its furnishings and ruins plundered. Near the church, there were many Christian tombs. After having them all opened, servants, slaves, and the riffraff exhumed the corpses that had been buried there and dispersed their bones, while dogs devoured the flesh from the recently buried bodies. Near the same church there was another, dedicated to Saint Cosma,

[16] Yahya al-Antākī, *Cronache dell'Egitto fatimide e dell'impero bizantino (937–1033)* [Chronicles of Fatimid Egypt and of the Byzantine Empire], ed. Bartolomeo Pirone, "Patrimonio Culturale Arabo Cristiano," ed. Samir Khalil Samir (Milan: Jaca Book, 1998), 3:246ff. (section 12:109 and 113).

[17] Ibid., 248 (section 12:116).

which belonged to the Jacobites [that is, the Copts]. They also destroyed it.[18]

The most serious episode—which provoked the violent military reaction of Christendom—was the destruction of the Church of the Resurrection in Jerusalem (called, in the West, the Church of the Holy Sepulcher), which began on September 28, 1009. Al-Ḥākim ordered his subjects to "make all symbols [of the Christian faith] disappear and to take away all venerated relics".[19] "The basilica was destroyed to its foundations, apart from what was impossible to be destroyed and difficult to take away. So the Place of the Skull, the Church of Saint Constantine, and all the other buildings included in its perimeter were demolished, while the holy relics were taken away. Ibn Abī Ẓāhir tried very hard to remove the Holy Sepulcher and to eradicate all traces of it and was able to tear down and abolish most of it."[20] One could go on talking at great length about the destruction of churches and other aggressions committed by Muslims against Christians.

Therefore, although the First Crusade was launched by the pope, it was not by any appeal to or a consequence of the Gospel. At that time, the pope represented the civil authority, and he made decisions regarding political and military questions. And this is a major point of difference.[21]

The Crusades were not considered wars of religion, not even by the Arab historians of those times. The Muslims

[18] Ibid., 248ff. (section 12:118–20).

[19] Ibid., 249 (section 12:122).

[20] Ibid., 249 ff. (section 12:122–23).

[21] Furthermore, the actions of the Crusaders can be studied and measured objectively by Christian criteria and judged as right or wrong deeds, and as good or sinful acts, but, as illustrated in the response given to the previous question, one cannot do the same with violent actions committed in the name of Islam, for these can be objectively justified by legitimate Muslim criteria.

never called them "Crusades", as they do today, in imitation of the West. The new Arab expression *al-ḥurūb al-ṣalībiyya* (the wars of those who hold the Cross), dates back only to the nineteenth century. Earlier, the Crusades were called *ḥurūb al-Faranj* (the wars of the Franks), which signified wars with the West in general.

The Arab historians sometimes specified the nationality of these Franks, talking about Germans, Hungarians, or Amalfitans. All these groups were regarded by the Arabs as distinct nations and peoples who arrived in the East to invade their land. Furthermore, during the Crusades, we often find Muslim princes making agreements with Frankish dukes in order to fight against other Muslim princes and Frankish dukes, as in all wars of interests.

Going back to *jihād*, we cannot consider the "military" interpretation as a falsification of Islam. But we can say that it is carried out only by some Muslims, which does not mean that it is less authentic. It is authentic but not exclusive.

28.   *Are there examples where the Muslim armies behaved peacefully during their conquest of some cities? For instance, during the conquest of Jerusalem in the year 636?*

This is another story. When the Muslim armies started to conquer the Middle East and large areas of Asia and Africa, they first needed to control the conquered lands, and only after that was achieved did they seek to convert their populations. Not always were conversions forced and immediate, in accord with the Arab proverb *Aslim, taslam!* (Embrace Islam and be safe!). The Muslim law is clear in this regard. The Muslim has the duty to announce to his enemy his intention of declaring war on him. If he refuses to submit, war is unavoidable, and the Muslim has the right to kill him because he has not surrendered. If, on the contrary, the other one would be ready to surrender, the Muslim would no longer have the right to kill him but only to occupy his land. In the first case, the non-Muslim can save his life only by becoming Muslim, because he was won through force. In the second case, there is not any obligation. These are the rules of war in Islam.

The obligation theoretically exists only when someone refuses to surrender to the political supremacy of Muslims. However, history shows that at the beginning, even though there was no such obligation, the outcome was the same. The occupation of Egypt, for instance, was carried out peacefully because the Egyptians surrendered and accepted to pay to Muslims the *jizya* (the head tax) and the *kharāj* (the tax on the land).

Increasingly more-burdensome taxes pushed many Christian Egyptians to become Muslims, and the same happened in many other Middle Eastern countries. Therefore, it is true that in the majority of cases, Muslims did not force the populations to convert to Islam. The constant pressures, both economic and social, pushed the majority of these populations to become Muslims in order to escape the taxes that Muslims used to fund new wars and conquests.

29.   *There is a particularly disturbing aspect about the relationship between Islam and violence that has dramatically resurfaced with recent incidents: that of the so-called martyrs who are the protagonists of terrorist attacks against the "enemies of Islam". The most informative incident was the suicide attack on the World Trade Center "Twin Towers" in New York City on September 11, 2001, but numerous other incidents took place in these intervening years, especially in Israel, by people who define themselves as "martyrs of Islam". Can we theorize that suicide in the name of Islam is permissible? And, from a Muslim point*

of view, is the name "martyr" for those who accomplish these actions correct?

In the Qur'ān, there is only one allusion to suicide, in Women, sura 4:29: "Believers, do not consume your wealth among yourselves in vanity, but rather trade with it by mutual consent. Do not kill yourselves. God is merciful to you." To this unique reference in the Qur'ān, a series of *ḥadīth* can be added: I know at least seven, and they all condemn suicide. One of these relates that the prophet of Islam refused to pray over a suicide's corpse; in another, it is prescribed that a suicide's corpse be burnt until only ashes are left, an abomination in the Muslim mentality. Definitely, suicide has no justification in the Muslim tradition; recently, however, the problem dramatically emerged because of the many episodes where terrorists chose to die in order to cause other people's death, claiming that they had done it for an "Islamic cause".

It is interesting to analyze some of the declarations that followed those events and that underline the importance that this debate has acquired in the Islamic world. Sheikh Muhammad Ṭanṭāwī, rector of al-Azhar University and considered one of the highest authorities in the Sunni world, in a *fatwā* pronounced on December 2, 2001, reasserted that suicide is to be condemned in every case. But some days later, another famous Egyptian sheikh, Yusūf al-Qaradāwī, accused Ṭanṭāwī of pronouncing abstract considerations and underlined his inability to apply classical rules to historical situations, such as the present one, where Islam is threatened in many parts of the world. According to Qaradāwī, "nobody can declare that it is unlawful to fight with all means against the [Israeli] occupation", and "*jihād* on the way to God and in the defense of the country, of homeland, and of sacred things is today an obligation for all

Muslims more than in any other period in the past ..., in Palestine, in Kashmir, and in other hot spots in the world."

This "theological discussion" was followed by an authoritative statement against the legitimacy of suicide by the deacon of the faculty of *sharīᶜa* at the University of Kuwait, Muhammad Ṭabaṭabā'ī. A few days later, the leader of the Shiite *ᶜulemā'* in Lebanon, sheikh Ḥabīb Nābulsī, legitimated the suicide attacks, declaring that the *fatwā* issued by Ṭanṭāwī "has no meaning and no legitimacy in Muslim jurisprudence because it does not refer to law but to politics and because his purposes are contrary to those of the *umma*" and therefore contrary to the true interests of Muslims.

On the same wavelength is the final document released at the end of the summit held in Beirut in January 2002, in which more than two hundred Sunni and Shiite *ᶜulemā'*, coming from thirty-five countries, participated: "The actions of martyrdom of the *mujāhidīn* are legitimate and have their foundation in the Qur'ān and in the prophet's tradition. They represent the most sublime of martyrdoms because the *mujāhidīn* accomplish them in full conscience and freedom of choice." In the document, the *ᶜulemā'* affirm that they are speaking "from their religious responsibilities and in the name of all peoples, rites, and countries of the Islamic nations" in order to give precise guidelines about the Palestinian cause.[22] According to the *ᶜulemā'*, the attacks should not be analyzed by themselves as acts of violence but according to the purpose for which they are committed—that is, they can be included in the category of *jihād* because a Muslim land in danger needs to be protected or liberated.

[22] Cf. Camille Eid, "Gli *ᶜulemā'* di 35 Paesi: Legittimi i kamikaze" [The *ᶜUlemā'* from 35 Countries: Kamikaze are Legitimate], *Avvenire*, January 13, 2002.

This perspective has found widespread acceptance in legitimizing the suicide actions. It also can be found in the field of education: many books used in Palestinian schools teach young people the obligation of *jihād* in all its forms and give legitimacy to the actions of those called "martyrs of Islam" by explaining that they must not be considered suicides but heroes who are destined for heaven because they made a true *jihād*. In fact, they behaved in conformity with the Qur'ān and sacrificed themselves for the Islamic cause. It is another example of the basic ambiguity of the Islamic world, which is unable to distinguish between faith and politics.

30.   *From the beginning of the twentieth century to the present day, the believers in Allah worldwide rose from 150 million to 1.2 billion. Christianity is still the largest religion, with more than 2 billion followers, but Muslims are the largest "confession", considering that, among Christians, Catholics are "only" 1.1 billion. Among the great religions, Islam is the one characterized by the highest expansion rate: the number of its believers grows 21.5 times faster than Christianity. What are the main reasons for this phenomenon?*

First of all, we must consider the high demographic expansion rate, which in Muslim countries is much higher than in countries with Christian culture: it is true that in the Western world, demographers have observed a progressive decrease of fecundity rates, but the effects of this will become obvious only in the coming decades.

Another important factor is missionary activity, the so-called *da'wa*, the task entrusted to every Muslim of propagating Islam among brothers of faith and in the rest of the world. It is a task especially undertaken by religious personnel fervently devoted to it but also by many zealous believers, and this produces many conversions in different parts of the world, including the Western countries.

It has been calculated that in Africa, the Muslim continent par excellence, for every person that converts to Christianity, seven convert to Islam. Three motivations in particular are at the basis of the rapid Muslim expansion in Africa. One is based on a common belief about so-called damages of colonization. The common idea is that Christianity is the religion of white people and is co-responsible for the colonization and later the dependency situation that these countries have endured, while Islam is the true religion of Africa. This subject impresses common people, but it is historically inaccurate and slanted because the first colonizers of Africa were Muslim, and the first slave dealers were Muslim; and this happened centuries before the European colonization and slave trade. The second motivation is based on the fact that Muslim habits are more similar to African native customs, such as polygamy, the submission of women, and a patriarchal concept of the family. The common African perceives that it takes less effort to be accepted in the Muslim religious community than to enter the Catholic Church. Christianity is more demanding. It often requires a long catechumenate period, which can last years before one is allowed to receive baptism.

A third motivation for the Islamic expansion is one that concerns not only Africa. I refer to the big funding campaigns that some countries (Saudi Arabia, several of the United Arab Emirates, and Libya) use to promote charitable, social, or cultural activities that attract many converts to Islam: the building of mosques, Islamic centers, qur'ānic schools, and radio and television stations; the supply of religious personnel; the opening of dispensaries and hospitals; and so on. All of this is very little known in Europe because Africa is rarely treated in European newspapers, but Islamic propaganda is, in fact, powerful, and in a few decades, if this trend remains unchanged, what in Africa is not Muslim yet will become so.[23]

The growth of Islam is also caused by discrimination at a juridical, economic, and social level, which is the reason for the emigration of thousands of Christians (or other non-Muslim groups) from some Muslim countries. Institutional changes, such as the adoption of *sharīʿa* in the penal code of some states in the Nigerian federation, caused vibrant but unheard protests by the local Catholic bishops and violent clashes in which thousands of people were killed and others fled.

There is naturally the presence of the religious-spiritual motivation that is at the basis of many conversions, especially in western Europe. This is simultaneously connected to the thirst for certainties and novelty in religious belief. Islam (and other religious belief systems, even Eastern mystical experiences) can be a fascinating answer to the human need for sacredness that is no longer satisfied by a certain "lukewarm" and moralistic way of life typical of modern-day Western Christianity.

D. Tradition and Modernity

31.   *The relationship between Islam and modernity is historically marked by a lack of comprehension, by diffidence, and by hostility. There are those who assert that Islam and modernity move according to two irreconcilable logics and that, in particular, modernity is perceived in the Muslim world as a typically Western phenomenon that threatens the integrity of tradition. What are the*

[23] See the three supplements of *AsiaNews* on *daʿwa* in the different continents, by Camille Eid and Carlo Broli, published by Pime, Milan 1999–2000.

historical reasons for this hostility? And what are the conditions that would open Muslim societies to the stimulus of laity and modernity without renouncing the foundations of their identity?

In order to understand the present dynamics of the relationship between the Islamic world, modernity, and the West, one must start at a period of history when the two worlds came into contact with each other after a long time of being far apart. This occurred during the transition from the eighteenth to the nineteenth century, in particular during Napoleon Bonaparte's campaign in Egypt (1798–1801). Egyptians discovered modernity and rediscovered European civilization through the work of scientists and technicians whom Bonaparte had brought with him: engineers, mathematicians, archeologists, astronomers, artists, economists, printers, pharmacists, and surgeons.

During that short period, the first book was printed in Egypt, titled *Exercises of Literary Arabic: Excerpts from the Qur'ān for Those Who Study This Language*, thanks to the Arabic characters brought from the print shop of Propaganda Fide in Rome. Studies were done on better ways to utilize the water of the Nile and on the construction of a channel connecting the Red Sea and the Mediterranean (a prologue to the future Suez Canal), as well as on the reform of the fiscal system and on the improvement of public education. The foundation of the Institute of Egypt helped gather into a single office the best intellectual and scientific resources in order to administer the country and lay the basis for future development. The results of all this work are reported in what has been described as a masterpiece of interdisciplinary collaboration, the *Description de l'Égypte*, ten volumes of texts and fourteen volumes of tables, published between 1809 and 1828.

After the French troops left Egypt, the governor, Muhammad 'Alī, considered the founder of modern Egypt, decided to continue on the same path. He sent cultured Egyptian men to Europe to study and specialize in different disciplines so that upon their return they could translate into Arabic what they had learned, in order to contribute to the modernization of Egypt's administration, economy, and society.

These were the beginnings of what would be named *Nahḍḍa*, the Arab-Muslim renaissance, which began in the second half of the nineteenth century and continued until the First World War and had Egypt as its fulcrum. There were three emblematic events of this process, and all took place on Egyptian soil: starting in 1860, the construction of the first railway of the Near East was followed by the opening of a university organized according to modern standards, and in 1870 the Opera House of Cairo was inaugurated with Verdi's *Aida*.

Hence, the Arab-Muslim world met the West, which appeared fascinating and shocking simultaneously. The West was fascinating because of its scientific, technological, and military accomplishments, which were superior to those that the Islamic civilization could produce; and the West was shocking because the Arab-Muslim world remained berthed on its past glory. It was this meeting that obliged the Arab-Muslim world to wake up abruptly and discover a dreadful reality.

32.   *Then might the situation be summarized with the question: How is it possible that the Muslim community, the one that the Qur'ān defines as the best in the world, can find itself in a condition of "backwardness" when compared to the West, and what are the causes of the cultural, scientific, and technological delay?*

To this question, many different answers can be given. The one advanced by the so-called Muslim reformers starting from the end of the nineteenth century ascribes the advance of the Western world as compared to the Muslim world to the ability to simultaneously develop science and a democratic system. But the reformers assert that these two systems are typically Muslim: the Qur'ān always favored science; there is even a saying: "Look for science, even if it were in China." Likewise, Muslim tradition always had what is called *shūra*, which is the "Council" (for consulting and then deciding together). Therefore, the reformers conclude that even democracy is an element that belongs to Islam.

It is through these points that the reformers (among the most prominent, I recall Gamāl al-Dīn al-Afghānī, renowned in the entire Muslim world; the Algerian Ibn Bādīs; the Egyptian Muḥammad ʿAbduh; the Syrian ʿAbd al-Raḥmān al-Kawākibī; and the Indian Muḥammad Iqbāl) were able to absorb some aspects of the Western world and integrate them into the Muslim tradition and promote them into legislative measures.

For example, at the beginning of the twentieth century, for the drafting of their constitutions, some nations of the Middle East patterned themselves on the Napoleonic Code and on the Swiss constitution by adapting them to the Islamic context. The greatness of the reformist movement that developed in that period consisted in its ability to absorb Western culture and civilization by reconciling them with the Islamic tradition.

But the years following the First World War represent a rupture in this process. The Ottoman Empire, the last major Islamic territorial domination in history, collapsed, and its holdings were fragmented—that is to say, its holdings were partly divided between England and France and partly inherited by new independent states. In 1923, a republic based on secular foundations was born in Turkey. This was a scandal for the classic Islamic mentality. Then in 1924, Mustafa

Kemal, the future Atatürk,[24] declared the fall of the khalifate, the unique authority recognized by the whole Islamic community. In reality, from the political point of view, the khalifate no longer had real weight, but it still had a strong symbolic and psychological meaning, and its end underlined the crisis of a system and of a vision of reality.

33.   *In the years between the two world wars, what happened to the Islamic conception of modernity?*

During this time, the process of reviewing, which had started at the beginning of the previous century, arrived at its fulfillment and at the same time changed meaning. The process of reviewing became a project for creating a new Islamic world, one free from all Western influence, a Muslim *sui generis* system. For example, in the twenties, Rashīd Riḍā (1865–1935), a disciple of the great Egyptian reformer Muḥammad 'Abduh (1849–1905), collected the messages and the writings of his master and published them in eight large volumes as a commentary on the Qur'ān titled *Tafsīr al-Manār* (The Interpretation of the Lighthouse, from the name of the magazine he founded, *al-Manār*). By doing this, he transformed the original perspective radically. He continuously quoted 'Abduh's statements (always referring to him as *al-ustādh al-imām*, the master *imām*), but he constantly explained them with his own rather fundamentalist ideas.

In 1928, one of Riḍā's disciples, Ḥassan al-Bannā (1906–1945), founded the Muslim Brotherhood (*al-Ikhwān al-Muslimūn*) in Egypt. From that single organization has come all the radical movements. Ḥassan al-Bannā traveled

---

[24] In 1934, the Grand National Assembly of Turkey bestowed on him the title "father of the Turks".

throughout Egypt, spreading the idea of the need to create a society based on the Qur'ān to transform Islam into a political community. When reduced to its essence, his message could be expressed as such: We will never beat the Western world if we try to imitate it; we need to create an Islamic project going back to a strictly literal interpretation of the Qur'ān. The vision can be summarized in his words: "The Qur'ān is our saber, and martyrdom is our desire. Islam is faith and cult, religion and state, Book and sword. As a universal religion, Islam is a religion good for any people and in any time of human history." The motto of the Muslim Brotherhood to this very day is "Islam is the solution."

Ḥassan al-Bannā's main disciple was Sayyid Quṭb,[25] who made a qualitative leap in his commentary on the Qur'ān titled *Fī-ẓilāl al-Qur'ān* (In the Shades of the Qur'ān) and in his book *Maʿālim fī al-ṭarīq* (Milestones): since the society we live in is violent and cannot be Islamized peacefully, Quṭb concluded that it is lawful to resort to violence. His stay in the United States, from November 1948 to August 1950, convinced him that only authentic Islam can save humanity from materialism and paganism. He is, in fact, the one who created the idea of *jāhiliyya* (the pagan ignorance) in order to describe modern non-Muslim societies. As Muhammad in his times had fought the pre-Islamic *jāhiliyya* by practicing the *jihād*—that is, by resorting to war— Sayyid Quṭb recommended doing the same toward the Muslim regimes that "betrayed" the Islamic cause. This is the

---

[25] Born in 1908, Quṭb was hanged on August 29, 1966, under Gamal Abdel Nasser, president of Egypt. About Quṭb's work, see the essay by Olivier Carré, *Mystique et politique: Lecture révolutionnaire du Coran par Sayyid Quṭb, Frère musulman radical* (Paris: Cerf, 1984). For the English edition, see *Mysticism and Politics: A Critical Reading of Fī-ẓilāl al-Qur'ān by Sayyid Quṭb (1906–1966)*, translated from the French by Carol Artigues and revised by W. Shepard (Brill, 2003).

reason the governments of the Islamic countries tried to eliminate the leaders of the Muslim Brotherhood, considering them subversive to the social and political order. Quṭb completed Ḥassan al-Bannā's vision by adding that Islam is necessarily called to fight if it wants to assume control and take the lead of mankind. Being a Muslim means being a warrior, a community of believers constantly in arms. The fighters who die in battle are martyrs for the faith because they put into practice the Law of God. The fight for God has no other purpose but God himself, to impose the divine order in the earthly world. The martyrs for the faith do not really die; they keep on living; they only change their form of life, as did Jesus, Son of Mary, who did not definitively die on the Cross.[26]

34.   *During the 1980s, there was the period of Khomeini and of the Iranian revolution, which seemed to have realized the hopes of the radicals for a return to a more authentic Islam. Were those hopes actually realized?*

For Islamic fundamentalists, the Iranian revolution, with the conquest of power by Khomeini in 1979, represents, in fact, the possibility of transforming into a political reality the dream of a society grounded on an authentic Muslim foundation. Today, even those who disagreed on the real application of Khomeini's dream still believe in that dream; and this conviction keeps feeding Islamic fundamentalism.[27]

At the present, Islamic fundamentalism has developed internationally but with a very different connotation. The

---

[26] See Sayyid Qutb, *Fī-zilāl al-Qur'ān*, vol. 11 (Cairo: Dār al-Shurug, n.d.), p. 117.

[27] The word "fundamentalism" was born in a Protestant environment, but it was later adopted by the Islamic world. In Arabic, the word *usūliyya* is used for fundamentalism, and *usūliyyūn* for fundamentalists.

moderate wing, for instance, asserts that although the Qur'ān must be the basis of Muslim society, it must be so in a modern version, without rigidity.

Another point of view proposes that the *sharīʿa*, the Islamic law organized in the tenth century by some great Muslim jurists, be considered as the basis of constitution and law.

There exists a third perspective, which represents the most radical Islamic thinking. It goes far beyond the conservative *sharīʿa* proposal by stating that the qur'ānic law must be imposed in any and all cases, even through violence. In order to realize this end, activists are trained in different countries in order to help spread these revolutionary ideas. Others who align with this tendency theorize about and practice terrorism. These groups include the Algerian GIA (Armed Islamic Group), who are responsible for attacks and for the slaughter of civilians, and Abu Sayyaf's group, which operates in the southern Philippine state of Mindanao. In Egypt, the Tanzīm al-Jihād group was responsible for the murder of President Anwar al-Sādāt on October 6, 1981. Operating within Egypt is al-Takfīr wa-l-higra (Anathema and Exile), founded by the Egyptian surgeon Ayman al-Ẓawāhirī. The physician became one of the best collaborators of Osama Bin Lādin and his al-Qāʿida organization.

The fundamentalists do not reject modernity, as some people mistakenly believe. On the contrary, they are ready to employ all modern techniques in order to spread their ideas, but they do not hold to the cultural categories of modernity. It is as if they harvested the fruits of a plant without understanding how to cultivate it. They refuse to follow the hard way to attain certain results because these would require a change of mentality. A change of approach to using reason and the modern analytical methods to understand reality is generally avoided. Such a change would produce a different view of the world from what can be deduced from the Qur'ān or from the *sharī'a*. As a result, the fundamentalists tend to keep letting religion, society, and politics overlap.

The radicals understand "modernity" to mean secularization, atheism, immorality, and paganism—in short, the Western enemy. Consequently, for them to accept modernity means putting their Muslim identity at risk or losing it. In conclusion, the problem is always the same: how is it possible to preserve one's individual and group identity while accepting the modern world and acting in it with a critical attitude? It remains a question of how Islam and modernity can be harmonized.

35.   *Nevertheless, especially in the past few decades, there have been multiple positions developed by liberal intellectuals, who try to reconcile faithfulness to the Qur'ān and to the fundamental principles of Islam with the historical-traditional development of modernity. What are the possibilities for acceptance of these enlightened positions? And can they have a real influence in the societies of the various Islamic countries?*

In this case as well, there exists a historical-theological premise from which one starts. For all Muslims, either conservative or liberal, the Qur'ān is not the work of Muhammad but of God himself. Therefore, it is timeless and not restricted to the seventh century; it is the word of God preserved, unchanged over time. The orthodox (and, with a particular emphasis, the fundamentalists) believe that each qur'ānic verse has an absolute value. In other words, it is valid at any time and at any place for every Muslim, regardless of the context, while the liberals propose a contextual reading and interpretation, taking into consideration place and time. Therefore, they emphasize the necessity of adapting the text to history, current events, and, in the final analysis, to modernity, a modernity that is not a synonym for atheism, immorality, and a denial of the religious dimension of life, as often occurs in the West.

And this is also what makes the work of the liberal groups so difficult in their respective countries: if modernity means the denial of religion, and if this is the message Europe and the West send out, it is difficult for the more-enlightened positions proposed in the Islamic countries to prevail. The governments, even those that seem very open to modernity, allow the radical tendencies to prevail for fear of losing the support of the Muslim masses. And the liberal positions, which have developed in different countries, remain chained and unable to "conquer" the lower classes and, in general, do not gain widespread acceptance.

III. The Challenge of Human Rights

A. *Sharīʿa* and Human Rights

36. *What is the foundation for human rights in Islamic culture?*

God is the source of all rights. In order to grant rights to man, God first of all expects the satisfaction of *his* right: man's complete obedience to the divine will, which, for a Muslim, is expressed in the Qur'ān and in the *sunna*. From these two principal sources is derived *al-sharīʿa* (the Muslim law, legitimized by revelation; hence, it is superior to any other law established by human initiative). Thus, *al-sharīʿa* is considered the perfect expression of divine will to grant men a means for the just regulation of human society.

Islam proceeds, therefore, from above: it comes from God's self-revelation in the Qur'ān and flows down to man and society. If the Qur'ān establishes the superiority of the husband over his wife, it is considered an unquestionable precept because it is the outcome of God's will. What appears to a Westerner as being contrary to women's rights and to the equality of the sexes is considered by Muslims as natural, just, and praiseworthy and as what most closely corresponds to the nature of man and woman; and it is good because God established it. And it is from this premise that a Muslim social and judicial system consistent with qur'ānic teachings has been built.

In Islamic thought, the argument of authority prevails ("God established this") over that of rationality ("reason allows man to reach the knowledge of moral law"). The qur'ānic norm is more authoritative than reality. Through the centuries, Muslim apologists have always attempted to demonstrate accordance between Islam and reason; they tried to prove that the statements contained in the Qur'ān are the best that can be thought for the good of humanity.

37.   *What are the basic characteristics of* al-sharī‘a?

Al-sharī‘a is founded on a threefold inequality: the inequality between man and woman, the inequality between Muslim and non-Muslim, and the inequality between freeman and slave. Apart from this last one, which is almost no longer found in practice, the other two are still valid.

They have their foundation in Arab history and culture. In the patriarchal society of Muhammad of the seventh century, the superiority of the man was an undisputed fact. Moreover, Muslims emphasize that the rights granted to women in Islam greatly exceed those that were in use in the pre-Islamic age: polygamy is accepted but limited to a maximum of four wives; a woman is provided with at least a part of the inheritance.

As regards inequality between Muslims and non-Muslims, Islam considers the former superior to the latter from the ontological and juridical point of view, even with regard to those that it defines as *dhimmī* (protected people), a term that refers to Jews and Christians. Tolerance granted to Jews and Christians does not imply equality with Muslims. Polytheists and atheists, on the other hand, enjoy no protection. Moreover, between the Islamic world and that of the "unbelievers" called *dār al-harb* (the House of War), there is theoretically a state of perpetual belligerence.

With respect to the protection of *dhimmī*, *al-sharī*ᶜ*a* bases itself on the prescriptions of the Qur'ān and on the agreements reached by Muslims with the populations subdued during the conquest of the Christian Middle East, starting with the agreement reached by Muhammad with the Jacobites of Najrān in 631 (year 10 of Hegira), which provided for the payment of a tribute by the Yemenite Christians in exchange for the preservation of their proper cult (their worship).

38. *The Universal Declaration of Human Rights is considered the primary reference document at the international level for any discussion of human rights. But when it was approved in 1948, it was criticized by leaders in many Islamic countries because it was regarded as the expression of a partial point of view. For what reasons?*

The Islamic countries question the universality of this declaration.[1] The rights expressed in the declaration are seen as a product of Western culture and of the political and economic ability of the West to impose its values on the international scene as valid for everybody. For this reason a document entitled "Universal Declaration of Human Rights in Islam" was issued during the proceedings of the Nineteenth Conference of the 45 Foreign Affair Ministers of the Organization of the Islamic Conference (OIC), held in Cairo in 1990.

In a certain sense, there is some truth in this Muslim reaction. The Universal Declaration of Human Rights is an expression of Western civilization and the culture of the

[1] The declaration was signed on December 10, 1948, by 44 nations. Many other countries signed later. A total of 171 nations took part in the World Conference on Human Rights held in Vienna in June 1993.

Christian world. Nonetheless, I think it is "universal", valid for everybody, because it reflects human nature. The fact that the West was the first to become aware of and to define these rights does not transform it into a partial document.

39.   *How are human rights expressed in the Cairo Declaration?*

First of all, the historical role of the *umma* (Muslim community) is reaffirmed, "the noblest community ever raised up for mankind".[2] Then the Cairo Declaration states that human rights are summarized by *al-sharīʿa*, the Islamic law, which is considered immutable and definitive, and that "all the fundamental rights and universal freedoms are part of the Muslim religion." This sentence is an expression of Muslim apologetics that systematically and a priori encompasses all existing values.

However, if one reasons from the general statements to specific applications, one finds declarations that seem to go in opposite directions. For example, "the father has the responsibility of the physical, moral and religious education of the offspring in conformity with his beliefs and his religious law" (article 19).

The omissions are significant as well: "Men and women have the right to marry without any restrictions as to race, color or citizenship." Religion is not mentioned because *al-sharīʿa* forbids Muslim women to marry non-Muslim men.

---

[2] The ʿImrāns, sura 3:110. For a detailed analysis of the documents produced on the subject of human rights in the Islamic world, see Maurice Borrmans, "Convergenze e divergenze tra la Dichiarazione universale dei diritti dell'uomo e le recenti Dichiarazioni dei diritti dell'uomo nell'islam" (Common Points and Differences between the Universal Declaration of Human Rights and the Recent Declarations of Human Rights in Islam), *Rivista Internazionale dei Diritti dell'Uomo* 12 (January–April 1999): 44–60.

Another important omission concerns freedom to change religion. This is solemnly stated in the United Nations declaration but is left out of the Islamic document, as it contradicts *al-sharīʿa*, which considers apostasy a crime.[3] Article 2 seems to admit religious freedom: "No one is authorized to limit the guarantees of religious freedom", but the text continues, "unless through Islamic authorities and in conformity with the provisions it [*sharia*] stipulates." Article 10 affirms that "Islam is the natural religion of man"; thus one must infer that it would be against nature to join another faith.

Article 10 envisages the institution of religious courts to settle the juridical questions of Jews and Christians, as it is stated by *al-sharīʿa* when it comes to the "problem" of *dhimmī*, the citizens "protected" by the Islamic state with a special statute.

The supremacy of the religious viewpoint is also reaffirmed by the last articles: "All the rights and freedoms stipulated in this declaration are subordinate to the Islamic *al-sharīʿa*" (article 24), and "The Islamic *sharīʿa* is the only source of reference for the explanation or clarification of any of the articles of this declaration" (article 25). Many chapters end with the restrictive expression "unless *al-sharīʿa* decides differently".[4]

It must be remembered that the Cairo Declaration was formulated not only in Arabic, with numerous qur'ānic and Islamic references, but also in two other official versions, in English and French, where the majority of the qur'ānic references and many other expressions were softened. One could

---

[3] See question 58, pp. 125–27 below.

[4] In joining the Convention on the Rights of the Child and the International Convention on the Elimination of All Forms of Racial Discrimination (CERD), Saudi Arabia expressed a reservation, namely, that the articles of the treaties do not contradict the Islamic law. See Amnesty International's report *Saudi Arabia: A Secret State of Suffering*, 2000.

say there exist two versions, one of which was formulated "for export" to the West.

40. *If a country is entirely Muslim, do you consider the application of qur'ānic law legitimate?*

I think that no religious law should become a civil law. It is as if a Christian nation or a society were ruled by the Church's canon law.

Even if the members of a population of Muslim countries belong to the Islamic faith by birth, culture, and tradition, everyone should have the freedom to adhere to Islam without any social or juridical obligation. The difference between a country like Italy and a 100 percent Islamic country is this: in Italy, if the citizen disagrees with a certain law, he has the possibility to struggle in order to change it and to create also a political movement for the purpose. However, in a country that takes *al-sharī‘a* as the constitution of the state—such as Saudi Arabia or Afghanistan under the Taliban—unjust laws are imposed, such as those regarding women, in the name of a hypothetical law established by God fourteen centuries ago. This is a form of violence first of all toward citizens who, even though Muslims, might hold different opinions.

The first victim of this system is freedom of thought. In many countries, the heads of the organizations that control publications are representatives of fundamentalist Islam who threaten the nonobservant writers and ban the books and magazines they consider harmful to the faith. As recently as 1997, the authorities of al-Azhar University in Cairo required the withdrawal of 196 books from use. These were most often books written by authors who try to revisit the Islamic tradition in order to give it more historical concreteness. I personally experienced this censorship at al-Azhar with the banning of three articles of mine dealing with critical editions of medieval Arabic texts that were to have been published in Christian reviews in Egypt.

41.   *What is the relationship between an individual's rights and the religious community of Islam?*

The individual is considered fully endowed with rights and duties only insofar as he belongs to the Islamic religious community. For this reason, those who abandon the community by converting to another religion or by becoming atheists are considered traitors and therefore lose their rights. In Christianity, on the contrary, it is the individual person who is endowed with rights. This conception is the basis of Western civilization and the juridical system that expressed itself in the Universal Declaration of Human Rights.

The Qur'ān and the Islamic tradition aim at protecting the Muslim community, not the individual. The condemnation of apostasy is justified by this principle: the good of the community prevails upon the good of the individual (and in this case, religious freedom). Even today, the Islamic world handles the relationship with Christians through the acknowledgment of the Christian community: if the community is not recognized at a juridical level, it is as if the Christians do not exist.

42.   *In the Islamic world, a lively discussion has been raised by those who urge the adoption of a position that is less chained to the literal interpretation of the Qur'ān and of Muhammad's sayings. What are the main expressions of this innovative development?*

I will try to offer a very simple analysis and explanation of a very complex and composite reality. I can identify two tendencies: one could be defined as pragmatic, and the other reformist, even on the theoretical level.

The first is seen in the political and juridical systems of some Islamic states that have introduced legal innovations departing from the classic Islamic law, accepting some "soft" progressive ideas about human rights. The most significant example comes from Tunisia, where there is the notable distinction between *al-sharīʿa* and family rights. Tunisian law grants equal rights to husband and wife and, with regard to offspring, overcomes the traditional privilege reserved for the man: polygamy is considered a crime, and repudiation of wives has been abolished. Some discrimination remains in the division of inheritance between male and female children. Also, a Muslim woman is not allowed to marry a non-Muslim: a ministerial disposition, in fact, forbids civil registrars to celebrate such a union.

More limited, but still significant, are some reforms that have been introduced in Morocco and Algeria, where a monogamy clause is admitted in marriage and where women are acknowledged the right of filing for divorce if this clause is broken. Moreover, the repudiation of a wife requires a court judgment, which denies validity to private pronouncement and requires the testimony of witnesses. The pragmatic tendency has the merit of allowing a small but progressive modernization of the law, even if it has the limitation of avoiding a confrontation that would challenge the culture with a new and modern interpretation of Islam, of the Islamic law, and of the law's foundations.

The aforementioned challenge, launched by a reformist tendency, is especially supported by some intellectuals. The position of the Tunisian Mohamed Talbi is emblematic because he makes freedom of conscience the fulcrum of his reflections. He starts with a reading of the Qur'ān that is no longer literal or fossilized but "with a purpose"—that is, capable of taking into account the historical context in which the Qur'ān was revealed and of capturing its real intentions in that context. Talbi concludes that freedom of conscience is a constitutional and inalienable right of human dignity, the "mother" of all other liberties. It is presented as the fundamental element of the anthropological vision proposed by the Qur'ān, without which no authentic act of faith is possible. Talbi traces back the main reason for the historical decline and the present difficulties of Muslim societies to the limitations imposed on fundamental liberties over the centuries. Thus his plea is to accept pluralism, which in his judgment is not foreign to, but reconcilable with, the most authentic spirit of Islam.[5]

Similarly, other enlightened intellectuals, whom Western public opinion or mass media generally ignore or follow in a detached way (and who should instead be encouraged in their difficult work of promoting modernization), are starting to move. Therefore, it was a good decision that the Fondazione Agnelli in Turin awarded to such a man as Talbi the first Senator Giovanni Agnelli Prize for Dialogue between Cultural Worlds (1997).

Another significant example of an enlightened intellectual is the Egyptian semiologist Naṣr Ḥāmid Abū Zayd. For twenty years, as a professor at the University of Cairo, he proposed interpreting the qur'ānic texts in relation to the historical and linguistic context of their times. According to Abū Zayd, the divine message is communicated through the linguistic code that is being used. Hence, it is not a literal revelation but an inspiration "translated" into the human language that can and must be studied and analyzed. Because of these academic ideas, Abū Zayd was accused

[5] A comprehensive illustration of Talbi's positions can be found in his book *Le vie del dialogo nell'Islam* [The Ways of Dialogue in Islam] (Turin: Fondazione Giovanni Agnelli, 1999).

of treating the Qur'ān as a historical text and therefore of denying its divine origin. In June 1995, he was condemned for apostasy, and the 'ulemā' of al-Azhar University asked the Egyptian government to apply the death penalty prescribed for apostate Muslims. Moreover, as he is no longer considered a Muslim, his wife lost the right lawfully to live with him. So they decided to go to the Netherlands, where Abū Zayd presently teaches Islamic studies at the University of Leiden.

43.   *What is the real impact of these positions on Islamic societies and institutions? To what extent do they succeed in breaking through common habits and mentality?*

This is very difficult to measure or evaluate, but one can look at these tendencies in action from two different perspectives. In the short run, we must admit that the pleas of the reformers have very limited influence over the formation of the Muslim mentality or social organization. But over time, their work is extremely precious because it proposes a model of reference for those scholars who seek instruments in order to reconcile Islam with the tensions and questions that characterize the social and cultural evolution of Islamic societies.

Apart from the work and writings of the reformist intellectuals is the significant and recent proliferation of movements for the defense and promotion of human rights in Muslim countries. These movements, even though faced with many difficulties, contribute to a pluralistic and democratic development. There are also groups that work for the emancipation of women, another part of Islamic societies that could help the process of modernization. Even the existence of Christian minorities, where they are allowed a certain freedom of expression, are in some cases an element that opens Islamic societies to modernity, as can be observed in the recent histories of Lebanon and Egypt. In the end, we should also remember the contributions given by "vituperated" and "evil" colonialism and by immigration to the West that put Muslims into contact with faraway worlds and civilizations. This process allowed many Muslims to become acquainted with Western juridical systems and to appreciate their validity.

44.   *What is the relationship between the civil and the religious law, between state and religion, both from the point of view of principles and of practical applications?*

Islam from its beginning presented itself as a global project that includes all the aspects of life. As pointed out above, in Arabic it is defined as *dīn wa dunya*, that is, religion and society, or *dīn wa dunya wa dawla* (religion, society, and state).

It includes a way of living and behaving; a way of conceiving marriage and family; a way of educating children; and even a way of eating. In this system of life, the political aspect is also included: how to organize the state, how to relate to other peoples, how to deal with war and peace, how to relate to foreigners.

All these aspects are codified on the basis of the Qur'ān and the *sunna* and have been preserved "frozen" for centuries, substantially impermeable from contact with history and with other sociocultural realities. Can Islam conceive itself in a different way? Will it ever be possible to distinguish religion from culture, society, or politics? This is the most radical challenge that Muslims are facing, even in our times, but what has happened until now causes them to be skeptical of the capacity for "rethinking" themselves, for accepting an open confrontation with history.

I have addressed these questions to different Islamic personalities many times, also in secular countries such as Tunisia, and they all answered more or less in the same way: many things can be separated, but the principle that Islam is *dīn wa dunya wa dawla* (religion, society, and state) cannot be touched. This is a real problem, even though I believe that, sooner or later, Islam will arrive at some sort of compromise because an increasing number of Muslims do not accept this way of thinking anymore. This uneasiness can be perceived and is expressed everywhere, especially in the movements of dissension from the ranks of the educated, as we have seen among the intellectuals.

A final remark: if the religious law determines the civil law and organizes the private and communal life of all those who live in a Muslim society or environment, and if this perspective remains unchanged—as is the case up to now—coexistence with those who do not belong to the Muslim community will necessarily be difficult. In a Muslim country, non-Muslims will have to submit to the Islamic system or else live in a situation of substantial intolerance. On the other hand, in the West or in non-Islamic countries, Muslims will find it difficult to adapt to the civil laws of these countries because they consider them foreign to their formation and to the rules of their religion.

Naturally, many adjustments can be found, and, as it is in the nature of every human being, there is the attempt to reconcile doctrine with necessities dictated by reality. Nevertheless, one must emphasize that as long as this rigidity at the level of doctrine is preserved, as long as the already-mentioned principle that Islam is religion, society, and state is considered untouchable, everything will remain very difficult to change.

45.   *What is the actual level of application of* al-sharīᶜa *rules? For instance, do the penal codes reflect the punishments indicated in* al-sharīᶜa?

Only a few countries in the Islamic world, such as Saudi Arabia, Iran, and Afghanistan (under Taliban rule), require the full application of the rules of *al-sharīᶜa*. Saudi Arabia does not even have a constitution. The Saudi authorities claim that the Qur'ān is its sole constitution. The majority of Islamic states, however, apply only part of *al-sharīᶜa*, usually the rules about family law.

The constitutions of these states and nations are often inspired by the European constitutions and are adapted to the Islamic situation, and this causes reactions on the part of the radicals. They demand the application of the entire Islamic law. In Egypt, the wording of the constitution was changed twice in the last thirty years in order to bring it closer to *al-sharīᶜa*. The first time it was changed, it stated that "*al-sharīᶜa* is the main source of the constitution"; the second time, it was altered to "the only source of the constitution". However, this is not true if one analyzes the individual articles; many of them are far from *al-sharīᶜa*. For example, Christians may serve in the military just like the Muslim citizens, and Christians are no longer required to pay the *jizya* (head tax) imposed on adult males or the *kharāj* (land tax) they were required to pay around a century ago.[6]

Fortunately, many Islamic legal prescriptions are no longer applicable. For example, if one considers the typical

---

[6] In April 1997, however, the leader of the Muslim Brotherhood, Mustafā Mashhūr, asked that Christians again be taxed and removed from military service. He expressed reservation over their reliability in the case of an attack against Egypt.

qur'ānic punishments known as *ḥudūd*,[7] one realizes that today the majority of Islamic countries ignores them due to their harshness and substitutes them with more-benign alternatives, including jail, fines, and beating. The crimes punished by the *ḥudūd* are theft, robbery, fornication, adultery, perjury, and the drinking of alcohol. Some countries also add apostasy to the list of crimes.

The typical qur'ānic punishments include cutting off a hand for a thief; cutting off a hand and a foot for a bandit; a hundred lashes with a cane for fornication; stoning for adultery; and crucifixion for apostasy. In many of the theft cases, the judge does not consider the value of the stolen property high enough to warrant the cutting off of a hand and will substitute some alternative punishment. In other cases, the fact that the convict committed the theft while the country was enduring a period of economic recession or because he was exploited by his employer is considered an extenuating circumstance. As can be seen, there is always the possibility of avoiding the application of the most stringent qur'ānic sanctions even when they are required in the penal code.

46. *Is it possible to find in the Qur'ān any counterinstructions to the aberrant principles of* al-sharī῾a?

The *fuqahā'* (the doctors of the Muslim law) show the same extraordinary ability (as do all lawyers and jurists throughout the world) in justifying almost any position. For example, if someone wanted to legitimize a lack of observance during Ramaḍān fasting, considered a very serious offense in Islam, he could refer to the same Islamic tradition. The

---

[7] The plural form of the Arabic word *ḥadd* (limit). The Qur'ān talks about the *ḥudūd Allāh*, meaning the "laws of God".

sunna allows, in fact, avoiding the fast during *jihād*. If it was declared, as the Tunisian president Bourguiba did in the past, that today the *jihād* is fought against ignorance and underdevelopment, which he considered the greatest enemies of Islam, in this phase of their existence Muslims could be excused from fasting. It is obvious that this is a juridical way out, but it is still passable. Tunisians did not follow their president's plea on this subject and remained loyal to the Ramaḍān fasting. Much, then, depends on the will of Muslims.

A way out is always possible, although the problem consists in creating a sufficiently developed conscience in the majority of the population in order to change things. A certain cultural level and much courage are needed to create a space between oneself and tradition, which is considered the supreme regulator of all aspects of life.

47.   *Did Turkey, commonly considered one of the most secular Islamic countries, succeed in achieving this goal?*

Only partially, for in that country the principle of secularization was imposed by Atatürk and was not asked for by the Turkish people. It is well known that in Turkey the true guardian of secularization and of the separation between Islam and politics is the army, not the civil institutions. As long as the generals and the supporters of this position are strong enough, the country will remain secular. During the last twenty years, however, Turkey has witnessed a rebirth of the Islamist tendency, represented by the Refah (Well-Being) party, which in the 1995 elections became the leading political party in the country,[8] taking its leader, Necmettin Erbakan, to the post of prime minister. At that point, the

---

[8] On that occasion, it won 158 out of 550 seats in the parliament.

military intervened to collapse the government, and Refah was dismissed by the Constitutional Court in January 1998, obliging its leaders to create another party, the Fazilet (Virtue) party.[9] This confirms that today the problem of secularization is still at the center of the political debate in Turkey, even though almost eighty years have passed since its implementation.

These two forces, the religious and the secular, are always in tension. During a recent journey to Turkey for an international meeting on Averroes (see p. 43), I noticed, on the one hand, the resumption of the once-banished call to prayer from the minarets, and on the other hand, a liberal approach to religious practices in the environments controlled by the state. I was struck by two facts: the first was that the organizers of the meeting (promoted by the Islamic theological faculty in Marmara) never interrupted the gathering to allow people time to attend ritual prayer; the second was that, during the breaks, only a very few people, ten at the most (one can tell from the number of shoes left at the door), attended the two *muṣallā* (Muslim prayer spaces) for prayer. Ten people out of approximately two hundred students, male and female, in an Islamic theological faculty are rather few.

Hence, the secularization of Turkey left a deep impression despite the strong popular opposition of many. Change in Islam is possible but very difficult. Christians went the opposite direction. The Gospel encourages the distinction between the religious and the political sectors of life when it directs Christians to render unto Caesar that which is Caesar's and unto God that which is God's. For centuries

---

[9] Led by Recai Kutan, in the 1999 elections the new party collected only 21.3 percent of votes, demoting it to third place in the Turkish political scene.

the two dimensions overlapped and mutually influenced each other, but we succeeded in separating them after a long crisis that culminated in the formulation of the principle of secularization. However, this is often misunderstood and taken as indifference (or even hostility) toward the religious dimension, as the Enlightenment thinkers wanted and as modern secularists propose. And it is precisely this misunderstanding or, better, this true degeneration that brings judgment and Muslim criticisms: "See what this separation of religion, society, and state has brought the West? It led to the dissemination of disembodied and abstract religion, to the loss of any transcendent reference above the material dimension, to a freedom with no points of reference, even to atheism."

I am more and more convinced that recovering an authentic secularization, which recognizes religion as a fundamental dimension of the human person and society that can be freely supported (but not imposed by the state, as normally happens in the Islamic countries), would be a great contribution to coexistence. It can offer an interesting reference point for those Muslims who try to combine democracy, freedom, and religious faith. This is a responsibility that the West, and Christians in particular, are called to fulfill in these years of radical changes.

B. The Condition of Women

48.   *Is it correct to say that in Islam, males are considered superior to females, or is this a commonplace but erroneous assumption of non-Muslims?*

The Qur'ān affirms the superiority of male over female, but the male's duty to protect the female is also clearly stated.

Verse 228 of the Cow, sura 2, affirms, "Men are superior to women" (literally, men "are a degree above" women), and verse 34 of Women, sura 4, says, "Men have authority over women because God has made the one superior to the other, and because they spend their wealth to maintain them." From these statements, a centuries-old tradition was established that gives the husband an almost absolute authority over his wife; this also is confirmed by the different *hadīth*.

I would like to draw attention to the fact that in Women, sura 4, the superiority of man is related both to the divine preference and to an economic reason, even if this second aspect is often ignored by exegetes and jurists. In essence, it affirms that the authority of the man derives *also* from the fact that the man maintains the woman. Is it correct to ask whether this authority is still valid when the man no longer maintains the woman? It happens more and more frequently today that the woman works and therefore is self-sufficient or is providing for the maintenance of her husband and family.

49. *Do you believe that there are similarities between the qur'ānic statements that establish authority of man over woman and some passages of the Letters of Paul in the New Testament?*

Asserting that Paul ascribes to man an authority over woman similar to that indicated in the Qur'ān is the result of a wrong reading of chapter 5 of the Letter to the Ephesians. Let us examine verses 21–33, which sum up the teaching and are often quoted in discussions about the relationship between husband and wife.[10]

[10] Here is the entire quoted passage:

Be subject to one another out of reverence for Christ. Wives, be subject to your husbands, as to the Lord. For the husband is the head of the wife as Christ is the head of the Church, his body, and is himself

The formal structure of these thirteen verses already indicates Paul's purpose. First of all, a general principle is declared: "Be subject to one another out of reverence for Christ" (v. 21). Then there are three verses (22–24) addressed to women, and another eight (25–32) directed to men. At the end is a final verse (33) that clarifies the attitude required of each of them. From this structure, one can deduce that Paul's words are an exhortation addressed to men more than to women.

To wives, Paul says that they must be subject to their husbands as the Church is subject to Christ. To husbands, Paul recommends that they love their wives "as Christ loved the Church and gave himself up for her"; five times he uses the verb *love*. And here is the conclusion: "However, let each one of you love his wife as himself, and let the wife see that she respects her husband."

Let us now examine the words in their historical context to see the originality of Paul's teaching. When he talks to women, he is not introducing a new precept: in fact, the Mosaic, the Hellenistic, and the Roman traditions had established the principle of the submission of women. The originality lays in the *how*, and Paul specifies that we must take

---

its Savior. As the Church is subject to Christ, so let wives also be subject in everything to their husbands. Husbands, love your wives, as Christ loved the Church and gave himself up for her, that he might sanctify her, having cleansed her by the washing of water with the word, that he might present the Church to himself in splendor, without spot or wrinkle or any such thing, that she might be holy and without blemish. Even so husbands should love their wives as their own bodies. He who loves his wife loves himself. For no man ever hates his own flesh, but nourishes and cherishes it, as Christ does the Church, because we are members of his body. "For this reason a man shall leave his father and mother and be joined to his wife, and the two shall become one flesh." This is a great mystery, and I mean in reference to Christ and the Church; however, let each one of you love his wife as himself, and let the wife see that she respects her husband (Eph 5:21–33).

as an example the submission of the Church to Christ, a love submission, a spiritual one, not the submission of a slave to her master. Therefore, in the conclusion, after clarifying the concept, he talks of "respect".

When he addresses husbands, he exhorts them to love their wives as Christ loved the Church by offering his life for her. In those times, as today, Paul probably noticed that there was a problem, a lack of love on the part of a man for his wife, and in this regard Paul said new things: you women, who are subject to your husbands, must act like the Church toward Christ, in a relationship of love; and you men, learn to love your wives. These are different forms of the same love.

The same perspective is used when Paul says that Christ was subject to the Father and obedient to him unto death, even death on a cross.[11] For the apostle, in this perspective, obedience and submission are not an act of degrading inferiority but an act of deference; evidence of this is the fact that Christ is not inferior to God but consubstantial with him.

In conclusion, while in the Christian conception man and woman are substantially on the same level, in the Muslim one an ontological difference is established, as is stated even today by Muslim authors who introduce the role of woman in Islam by explaining that "being by her nature physically weaker, psychologically more fragile, and more emotional than rational, she is inferior to man and therefore must be submitted to him."

50. *How is the theory of woman's inferiority to man translated into practice?*

Here I am not referring to the inequalities that may exist at a *sociological* level between men and women that can be

[11] See Phil 2:8.

verified in daily life. Unfortunately, these inequalities are widespread in all societies, cultures, and civilizations and are very much present in the Islamic world. Instead, I want to talk about the *juridical* inequality, which has lasting consequences because it is normative. It often hinders or in any case delays any adequacy of the mentality of today's Muslim men and women.

Obviously my remarks are very general because an analytical investigation of the situations in each different country is not possible here.

1. First, there is *inequality in the possibility of getting married*. The male is acknowledged the possibility of having up to four wives at the same time (polygamy). At the same time, a woman is denied the possibility of being married to more than one man simultaneously (polyandry). Legal polygamy establishes a state of radical inequality between males and females. It causes a male to believe that women are made for his pleasure, and to the extent that his wife is one of his properties, he can "plow" as he likes, as is literally stated in the Qur'ān.[12] If the male has the economic means, he "buys" another one. The woman is in a condition of submission, and her role is to be an object of pleasure and reproduction; this role is reinforced by the fact that in the Qur'ān, with one exception, she is never known or even called by her proper name but in relation to a male: daughter of ... , wife of ... , mother of ...[13]

2. *A Muslim woman may not marry a man of a different faith*, unless he first converts to Islam. This prohibition derives from the fact that in the patriarchal Eastern societies, the

[12] See the Cow, sura 2:223: "Women are your fields: go, then, into your fields whence you please."

[13] In the Qur'ān, except for Mary the Mother of Jesus, no woman is mentioned by proper name. They are all named by referring to the family relationship they have with a man.

children always adopt their father's religion.[14] It is also justified by the fact that the father is the guarantor of the religious education of children; therefore, only if he is Muslim can he provide for their training according to Islamic principles. In this regard, I would like to emphasize the fact that children born of a Muslim parent are considered Muslims, even if they are baptized into another religion. Therefore, all mixed marriages (between a Muslim male and a Christian female or between a Muslim male and a Jewish female, which are the only two cases addressed in *al-shari'a*) increase the Muslim community numerically and at the same time diminish the non-Muslim community.

3. *The husband can repudiate his wife* by repeating the sentence "You are repudiated" three times in the presence of two adult, mentally sound Muslim males, with no referral to a legal tribunal. The most absurd thing is that if the husband later repents of his decision and wants to "recover" his wife, she must first marry another man who in his turn will repudiate her.[15] In that case, the woman passes from hand to hand in order formally to respect the law. A wife cannot repudiate her husband. She can ask for divorce, but it becomes for her a cause of shame and puts her in a very fragile sociological situation. In any case, the repudiation is experienced as a humiliation for the woman because people infer that she has physical or moral defects.

---

[14] In Judaism, on the contrary, it is the mother who transmits her religion to the offspring for reasons connected with the waiting for the Messiah, because the Messiah must necessarily be born of a Jewish woman.

[15] See the Cow, sura 2:229–30: "Divorce [revocable divorce, or the renunciation of one's wife on oath] may be pronounced twice, and then a woman must be retained in honor or allowed to go with kindness.... If a man divorces his wife [by pronouncing the formula "I divorce you" for the third time], he cannot remarry her until she has wedded another man and been divorced by him."

Finally, the ease with which a husband can repudiate his wife without having to justify his decision makes her totally dependent on his mood. A Muslim wife lives with the constant fear of being sent away. It is like the "sword of Damocles" suspended over her head: if she does not behave according to her husband's desires, she could be repudiated, and then she would have to look for another male who would accept and take her as a wife.

4. In the fourth place, we must consider *the easiness with which a male-requested decree of divorce is obtained.* Traditionally, there is not even the need of going to a tribunal. It is true that one of Muhammad's *ḥadīth* says that "divorce is the most hideous among lawful things", but it is permitted nonetheless.

5. The *custody of children,* following the divorce, is another example of inequality. The children "belong" to the father, who decides on their education, even if they are temporarily entrusted to the mother until they reach age seven. Only the father has legal authority.

6. There also is the issue of *inheritance.* A female has the right to half the inheritance of a male,[16] a rule that is founded on the socioeconomic situation in which the family lived in ancient times. According to the Qur'ān, since it is the man who has the duty of maintaining the woman and the entire family, it is logical that he needs a small fund he can tap for expenditures. Even in this case, an inequality established by divine law increases the dependence of woman on man.

7. The seventh difference from a juridical point of view is that *the legal testimony of one man is worth that of two women.*

[16] "God has thus enjoined you concerning your children: A male shall inherit twice as much as a female" (Women, sura 4:11); "If he [the deceased man] has both brothers and sisters, the share of each male shall be that of two females" (Women, sura 4:176).

This is based on one of Muhammad's *ḥadīth* that has very widespread acceptance in Muslim environments despite its doubtful authenticity. It affirms that "woman is lacking in faith and intelligence". When you ask the *fuqahā'* (the experts of the Muslim law) to explain the reason for that statement, they answer that woman is lacking in faith because, in some situations (for instance, during her menses), her prayer and her fasting are not valid and her religious practice is therefore lacking. With regard to the second part of the affirmation, the "imperfection" in intelligence, perhaps in the past this could be explained sociologically by recalling that women were less educated, studied less, were less involved in social life, and were devoted only to housework. Nowadays, this is no longer the case. Nevertheless, in the majority of tribunals in Muslim countries, this principle is still in force, despite the protests of feminist associations. In some countries, the fundamentalist Muslims demand that women be forbidden to testify in trials where qur'ānic punishments are involved.

8. One last difference—and perhaps the most serious one for its practical consequences—concerns daily life and establishes that *a husband has* absolute authority *over his wife*.[17] A husband has the obligation of correcting her behavior by physical beating until she obeys.[18] A man can forbid his wife to go out from the home, even to go to the mosque, since in a *ḥadīth* Muhammad tells a woman that her prayer has no value if it is done without her husband's permission. Paradoxically, in this case obedience to the husband has more value than obedience to God. All these juridical rules make

---

[17] See Women, sura 4:34: "Men have authority over women."

[18] See Women, sura 4:34: "As for those from whom you fear disobedience, admonish them, forsake them in beds apart, and beat them. Then if they obey you, take no further action against them."

the Muslim woman a person deprived of the same rights as the man.[19]

51.   Can we talk of the requirement for the woman to wear a veil?

For the majority of Muslims, the requirement for a woman to wear a veil in public is not a juridical question but a question of local custom, while according to the interpretation of the radicals the wearing of a veil is an obligation that derives from the Qur'ān. The juridical basis of this measure is supposed to be verse 31 of Light, sura 24:

> Enjoin believing women to turn their eyes away from temptation and to preserve their chastity; not to display their adornments (except such as are normally revealed); to draw their veils over their bosoms and not to display their finery except to their husbands,[20] their fathers, their husbands' fathers, their sons, their husbands' sons [stepsons], their brothers, their brothers' sons, their sisters' sons, their women-servants, and their slave-girls; male attendants lacking in natural vigor, and children who have no carnal knowledge of women.[21] And let them not stamp their feet when walking so as to reveal their hidden trinkets.

---

[19] For a deeper analysis of the juridical and sociological aspects of marriage in the Islamic culture, see Roberta Aluffi Beck-Peccoz, *Le leggi del diritto di famiglia negli Stati arabi del Nord-Africa* [The Regulations of Family Law in the North African Arab States] (Turin: Fondazione Giovanni Agnelli, 1997), and Giancarla Perotti Barra, *Sposare un musulmano: Aspetti sociali e pastorali* [Marrying a Muslim: Social and Pastoral Aspects] (Cantalupa [Turin]: Effatà, 2001).

[20] The Arabic word used here (three times in the verse) is *ba'l*, which means "master", as does "Baal" in the Bible.

[21] The described figures correspond to what, even today, the Bedouin tradition calls the *Maḥārim*.

Many Muslim jurists claim that the order to hide some parts of the face and the body was given only to Muhammad's wives. There is an age-old controversy among Muslims based on the context of the revelation (in Arabic, *asbāb al-tanzīl*) of this obligation. According to some commentators, it derived from the excessive freedom that some of Muhammad's wives took with the men who came to visit the prophet.[22] He seems to have been shocked by this behavior and to have received from heaven a whole verse that halted this embarrassing situation. From this original intention of limiting the veil to the wives of the prophet, the obligation was then extended to the "wives of the believers", as verse 59 of the Confederate Tribes, sura 33, states: "Prophet, enjoin your wives, your daughters, and the wives of true believers to draw their veils close round them. That is more proper, so that they may be recognized and not be molested."

According to what the scholars of Arabic sources claim, the rule of the veil was not rigidly applied to other women, who were free to follow it or not. The so-called *musfirāt* (unveiled women) were a large number at the time of the prophet. Also in this case, the basic problem is that in the Muslim world there is a tendency to consider anything as holy, through the authority of the Qur'ān, what in different contexts is considered only a tradition or a custom. In Cairo, the most inhabited capital of the Arab world, the majority of women did not wear the veil until thirty years ago. Then a wave of rigid application of this qur'ānic prescription arrived, favored by the Muslim radicals.

In any case, for Muslim jurists, the definition of what must be veiled is not clear. The Arab word *khumūrihinna* (which

---

[22] Different *ḥadīth* talk about the revelation of the verse of the veil on the occasion of Muhammad's marriage (the seventh) with Zaynab bint Jaḥsh, former wife of Zayd, adopted son of the prophet. During the wedding banquet, some men seem to have talked with her.

is translated as "their mantels") suggests that the face is not included in the prohibition. Hence there are a variety of female Islamic garments, from the simple *foulard* that covers just the hair, to the *ḥijāb* that covers the woman along the whole body, including the wrists and the ankles, and covers the zone of the bosom from the breast to the neck and hair, leaving uncovered the hands, the face, and in some cases, the feet. Then there is the *chador*, in black, which also includes gloves for the hands, very widespread among Shiite women, and the *burqa* (from the Arabic *burquᶜ*), which was imposed by the Taliban upon all Afghan women and which covers them completely, leaving a small opening for the eyes, which are covered by a net or by the *niqāb*, a veil on the face. These garments are not prescribed by the *sunna* or the Qur'ān, however. In actual fact, women do not have a choice due to social pressure.

52.   *How is actual discrimination against women experienced in the Muslim countries?*

It is difficult to offer a general summary statement on this issue. One can say that the level of discrimination experienced by females depends on culture and tradition. Among the masses, the requirement of submission is accepted insofar as the woman has always witnessed her mother submit to her husband; hence, it is easier to follow in her mother's footsteps. Among the more cultivated, if the husband has a traditionalist mentality, the situation of the wife is more difficult and more unacceptable the more she is educated, is open to modernity, is connected to the working world, or has experiences outside of the family circle.

When a Muslim family lives in the West, as in the case of immigrants, the daughter attends school, as does the son; she learns the same things; she studies the same subjects; she normally has male friends; and she lives more or less like her classmates. Then, when she reaches adolescence, she cannot understand why her family suddenly blocks her public life. For adults, if the qur'ānic motivation for the protection of women is based on their maintenance by men, then this principle no longer has meaning today in modern society for the wife who works at a job outside the home and, in some cases, earns more money than her husband, or even maintains him. Would the man accept submission to his wife and pass on to her his authority if she were the one who maintained the family? It is clear that in these situations, there is a conflict between the rules of Islam—which are considered immutable, as the radicals want—and the impact of societies that propose habits that are in contrast with them.

In the case of the young, the daughter submits to her family but feels frustrated and asks, "Why did they let me study?" or she decides to rebel against the rules that she has been taught since her childhood. Then she risks another kind of frustration because she will be regarded as a woman who rejected her faith and her cultural traditions by "surrendering" to the value system of the country to which her family immigrated. It is the common generational conflict experienced by all immigrant parents and their children, who live between two cultures. The parents seek to maintain the old cultural traditions in private family life, while their children want to engage fully in the new culture of their new country. It makes for very real conflicts within families between cultures and civilizations.

53. *What about the rules that regulate mixed marriages, a phenomenon that has been growing in recent years due to immigration and to the improved possibility of traveling on an international level?*

The most important aspect is that these marriages are always in the same direction because a Muslim man may marry a non-Muslim woman, but a Muslim woman may not marry a non-Muslim man, unless he first agrees to convert to Islam.

These mixed marriages have multiplied, but in many cases they fail because of the conflicts that develop between the spouses. In Islam, marriage is not a sacrament, as in Christianity, but a contract between a man and a woman (the latter represented by a guardian, *walīy*). Mixed marriages involving Muslims create problems not only for Christians but for all Westerners. In fact, the manner of organizing married life is different in Islam, as is the vision of sexual intercourse, in which the woman must always be available for the man. The "contract" specifies the rights and duties of each spouse: the man provides for the family needs, and the woman is responsible for the smooth functioning of the household.

In a mixed marriage, the wife legally loses the right to her husband's inheritance if she does not convert to Islam. In case of separation, the children belong to their father, although the mother is in charge of taking care of them until the children reach the age of seven years maximum. With regard to the obligations following the separation, Muslim law obligates the husband financially to maintain his estranged wife for nine months. This is for the simple reason that if she has recently conceived a child by him, he would be obligated to educate and support it. However, if this temporal period passes without the birth of a child, the man can serenely go his own way.

Although some states like Tunisia have started a process of modernizing family law by eliminating some inequalities, we must admit that the condition of women in Islam, both at a juridical and at a practical level, remains very penalized today.

54.   *One of the most controversial and dramatic aspects of mixed marriages is the destiny of children in the case of conflicts*

between husband and wife. It is not rare that Muslim husbands move back to their countries, taking the children away from their mothers and obtaining from the tribunals of their countries the authorization to keep them.

The problem arises when the marriage is contracted between a Western woman and a Muslim man—an Egyptian, for instance. The typical example is the journey of the husband to his native country. The children are brought along on the pretext of spending the holidays there with his family. This action is followed by his refusal to go back to the West. It is sadly the case, but it becomes impossible for the wife to recover her children because the laws of those countries always favor the Muslim spouse. The Egyptian law even establishes that children must belong to "the better religion", meaning Islam. This is another example of discrimination based on religion.

55.   *In conclusion, is it possible to hope for an improvement of women's rights in Islam?*

This is possible only if a program of education on the rights of the human person is introduced and developed. Such a program will have to promote equal opportunities for males and females. This process of change would be equivalent to a real cultural revolution and might be able to change the mentality of the sheikhs, the religious authorities. At this moment in history, the possibilities for significant change are most discouraging because the conservative positions of the authorities in Islamic countries prevail.

Another source of change is the human rights movements and the organizations that strive for the emancipation of women in the Muslim world. These groups are still a minority, with little influence on the general population.

The appointment of the Pakistani Muslim woman Irene Khan to head the Amnesty International organization in August 2001 might give an impulse to the promotion of women's rights in the Muslim world.

There are some important female figures in the literary, artistic, and entertainment fields, but their words reach only a very limited audience and have more of an impact on the Western world than on their own countries. Moreover, some of these female characters claim an emancipation inspired by Western models, but it is completely dissociated from the Muslim tradition. This factor certainly does not further the penetration of the women's message among the common people.

In this case as well, the relationship with the West turns out to be crucial in two opposing ways. It can positively influence the difficult process of evolution of the current condition of Muslim women by showing that the improvements obtained in Western societies in the name of the dignity of woman need not be feared. Yet the relationship with the West also can lead to a rejection of models that transmit a degraded image of the body and of sexuality. In these models, the sacredness of life and the respect of certain values, which are the basis of both Islamic and Christian anthropologies, are set aside for the myths of materialism, consumerism, and a false sense of freedom that closely resembles libertinism.

C. Religious Freedom and Apostasy

56. *In the area of religious rights and freedoms, one of the most controversial topics is the one related to the freedom of professing a faith different from Islam inside a Muslim country. How is religious freedom conceived in Islam?*

The idea of religious freedom is very peculiar: while Jews and Christians may profess their faith according to the qur'ānic prescription with regard to the "people of the Book", those who follow other religions have no rights. During the Muslim expansion in the Middle East (in the seventh and eighth centuries), this stipulation produced "protection treaties" with the different Christian communities that wanted to regulate the status of the *dhimmī* (protected people) in the conquered regions. These treaties granted the safety of people and properties and religious freedom, but they often imposed prohibitions and signs of inferiority. In exchange for the Islamic protection (the *dhimma*) offered by Muslims, Christians could keep professing their faith, but they had to prove their loyalty toward the authorities by acknowledging the superiority of Islam and by paying the *jizya* (the head tax).

During the centuries since these provisions were granted, a gradual, peaceful Islamization of the conquered countries took place. In fact, obstacles were imposed on non-Muslims, such as restrictions on public religious practices (including the ringing of church bells, processions in the streets, and the exposition of Christian symbols). There were also prohibitions against the construction of new churches and the restoration of ruined ones. The exercise of apostolic activity among Muslims was prohibited, although no resistance or interference with Muslim activity to convert the Christians was allowed. Other impediments were of a social nature, such as the refusal to allow Christians to have a political or military career, to marry Muslim women, and to give testimony in front of tribunals.[23]

The system of *dhimma* was therefore experienced as a humiliating domination, and with time, it became more and

---

[23] Nevertheless, it must be remembered that during the Muslim empire, some Christians performed official duties, which still happens today in some countries with a Muslim majority.

more unbearable. Christians could be professionally success-
ful, but their "inferiority" was fundamentally established in
the eyes of the Muslims. Their success appeared illegiti-
mate, and their exercise of any kind of power appeared abnormal. In daily life, Christians were forced to accept continuous
humiliations that were meant to remind them of their inferior condition, in conformity with the qur'ānic text that
orders Muslims to fight the people of the Book "until they
pay tribute [*jizya*] out of hand and are utterly subdued." [24]
In moments of crisis, it is against Christians that Muslim
hatred is concentrated, and Christians are made scapegoats
by the authorities, while during wars, they are suspected of
connivance with the enemy.

57.   *Today the majority of non-Muslims in Muslim countries
are Christians: there are about ninety million Christians living
with nine hundred million Muslims.* [25] *What level of religious freedom are Christians granted?*

The situation of religious freedom differs from one Muslim
country to another. We go from the prohibition of display-
ing religious symbols on the buildings or even on the body
(for instance, wearing a cross around the neck), to legal
obstacles to the profession and propagation of the faith, to
restrictions on the construction or restoration of worship
centers, to the prohibition against celebrating Mass privately or of introducing into a Muslim country any non-
Muslim religious texts. To a large extent, the differences
depend on the political, cultural, and national context, as
well as on the size of the Christian presence. In fact, there

[24] Repentance, sura 9:29.
[25] Of these Christians, 14 million are in the Arab countries, 40 million
are in Nigeria, 20 million are in Indonesia, 3 million are in Pakistan, and
smaller numbers are in Chad, Malaysia, and Central Asia.

are countries where the percentage of Christians in the national population is high, and others where it is very low;[26] there are countries where the *sharīʿa* is applied, others where Islam is declared as the state religion, and other places that opted for a certain degree of secularization; there are countries where Christianity is considered an indigenous reality, such as in Egypt, Lebanon, Jordan, Iraq, Syria, and Palestine, and other lands where it is professed by foreign communities, as in Maghreb and in the Gulf states.

The country with the most restrictions on religious freedom is Saudi Arabia, which forbids all non-Islamic worship because Saudi Arabia is considered the Muslim "holy land". With this expression, the Saudi authorities, as guardians of the two holy cities of Islam (Mecca and Medina),[27] declared that the whole territory of their country is comparable to a mosque, and therefore the presence of religious symbols different from the Islamic ones is not permitted. Among the six million foreign workers, at least six hundred thousand are Christians, and they cannot celebrate any form of religious worship, not even privately. The participation in clandestine prayer meetings, as well as the possession of non-Islamic religious objects, including Bibles, rosaries, crosses, and holy images, is liable to be punished with arrest and expulsion, or even with death.

The situation of Christian foreign workers in the other Gulf countries is a little better: authorities permit a limited freedom of worship and of ecclesiastical organization and sometimes allow the building of churches. Yet the Christian communities are constantly reminded to avoid any form

[26] The percentages are 40–45% in Lebanon; 40% in Nigeria; 35% in Chad; 8–10% in Egypt, Indonesia, and Sudan; 8% in Syria; 4% in Iraq; 3% in Pakistan, and less than 1% in Turkey, Iran, and North Africa.

[27] In fact, the official title of King Fahd of Arabia is that of "servant of the two holy places" (*khādim al-ḥaramayn al-sharīfayn*).

of evangelical or apostolic works among Muslims. In the North African countries, Christians are organized into dioceses and enjoy freedom of worship, but they must exercise certain discretion for reasons connected with the colonial past.

In Muslim countries with a native Christian population, the situations are different. In some places, such as Sudan, repression is authorized or led at an institutional level, with a government that calls for *jihād*, supports the ethnic-cultural conflict that currently rages in the nation's south, and supports forced conversions to Islam in the refugee camps. Another case of open discrimination is that of Pakistan, where Christians for years have been urging the withdrawal of the law on blasphemy[28] and the revision of pro-Muslim legislation. In many countries of the Middle East (such as Syria, Iraq, Egypt, Jordan, and Iran), the participation of Christians in the social, cultural, and sometimes political life of the country is protected, with some limits and restrictions. In this case, the unfailing tensions can be related to cultural factors or to the political situation (as in the Palestinian problem or the embargo against Iraq) or to the growth of the phenomenon of fundamentalism. In Lebanon, the fundamental role of Christians in the different fields of national life and Christians' equality in parliamentary representation along with Muslims are established by the constitution, even though the agreements of Ṭā'if (Saudi Arabia, 1989) considerably reduced the political power of Christians and compromised an already-fragile confessional balance.

[28] The law punishes with death those accused of offending Muhammad and condemns to life imprisonment those who offend the Qur'ān. Despite the guarantees to defend the rights of minorities, abuses by individuals or Islamic radical groups are frequent. This law of capital punishment, condemning converts from Islam, continues to be in effect to the present day.

58.   *Islam forbids Muslims to convert to another religious faith,
and the consequences of this transgression are very serious. What
are the theological and juridical foundations of this rule and the
punishments for those who break it?*

According to a well-known *ḥadīth* of Muhammad, every
man who is born on earth is born Muslim; it is his parents who impose on him a different religion (Jewish, Christian, Buddhist, Hindu, etc.). The conversion of a Muslim
to another faith is therefore considered a serious mistake
and a betrayal of the community of true believers, the *umma*,
where one can only enter and from which one is forbidden to leave. The duty of every Muslim is to invite all
men to convert to Islam, and this is a fundamental aspect
of *daʿwa*, the mission of announcing the truth to all of
humanity. Religious freedom in every Muslim nation is
conceived as freedom to adhere to true religion—that
is, to Islam—while the conversion to another faith is considered something unnatural and therefore is severely
prohibited.

Let us start by considering some Arabic terminology. *Ridda*
and *murtadd* are the terms that define apostasy and the
apostate, which is the Muslim who repudiates his faith. The
prevailing tradition asserts that the punishment to be inflicted
on the apostate is death. Historically, this practice was so
widespread that sometimes, in order to eliminate an inno-
cent man, he was accused of apostasy.

What does the Qur'ān say about this? Out of fourteen
verses condemning apostasy, thirteen contemplate "woeful
punishment in the world to come", and only one (in Repentance, sura 9:74) states that "God will sternly punish them,
both in this world and in the world to come." All the commentators admit that this reference is too vague to make us
think of a specific punishment, if we consider that for theft

or for adultery the Qur'ān prescribes very precise sanctions. We are surprised by the fact that, in order to condemn so serious an offense with such a severe punishment as the death penalty, a very generic allusion is sufficient for legal scholars: "God will sternly punish them, both in this world and in the world to come."

The fundamentalists always refer to two arguments. The first is of juridical character, based on the issuance of a *fatwā* by jurists who were capable of justifying their declarations from an Islamic point of view; the second is founded on historical arguments, based on the so-called apostasy wars, in Arabic *ḥurūb al-ridda* (literally "the wars of return", which implies the return to paganism), led by the first khalif, Abū Bakr. In this case, however, it is clearly an instrumental interpretation. Here, in short, are the facts: when Muhammad died, many Arab tribes that had submitted to him and that paid a heavy tribute as a sign of alliance refused to keep paying it. Abū Bakr led various military campaigns against them and succeeded in forcing many under his dominion again. It is clear, for the contemporaries of the khalif as for Muslim historians, that these wars had economic and political causes and aims, not religious ones: the tribes that had declared their independence had to be forced back under the domination of the khalif and not be punished for a religious betrayal. Moreover, liberal Muslims underline that Muhammad never directed anyone to kill an apostate; in fact, he intervened on two occasions to prevent his followers from killing individuals who had publicly abandoned Islam.

Definitely, the recourse to the death penalty does not seem to have acceptable qur'ānic foundations. However, one has to admit that in the *ḥadīth* tradition, the death penalty for apostasy does exist; for example, it is reported that the messenger of Allah said, "Whoever changes his religion, kill him."[29] One must also admit that the practice is established historically. During the last few decades, the so-called Islamic awakening, it became tragically frequent because the supporters of the radical currents brought pressure on authorities to enforce laws declaring that anyone who abandoned Islam would be severely punished. Therefore, some countries introduced into their constitution or into their penal code the offense of apostasy. This action is openly in opposition to the Universal Declaration of Human Rights of 1948 and is also repulsive to the conscience of many Muslims.

59.   *Could you give us some examples of how apostasy is punished?*

The most recent example comes from Afghanistan, where the Taliban regime, which ruled the country from 1996 to 2001, introduced the death penalty for all those who converted to religions other than Islam.

Article 126 of the penal code of Sudan of 1991 states:

Any Muslim who makes propaganda [any public display of conversion, open evangelization, etc.] in order to leave the Islamic nation [*millat al-islām*] or who openly declares his abandonment with an explicit declaration or with an action that has an absolutely clear meaning, commits the crime of apostasy. Those who commit the crime of apostasy are invited to repent in a period of time established by the tribunal. If he persists in his apostasy and does not come back to Islam, he will be punished by death. The punishment for apostasy ceases if the apostate retracts prior to his execution.

Saudi Arabia has always considered apostasy a crime to be punished with the death penalty. Its constitution is the Qur'ān

---

[29] Cf. Ṣaḥīḥ Bukhari 9:84:57.

and is interpreted in a rigorous way according to the Wahhabi tradition.

The 1993 reformation of the penal law in Kuwait provides for the death penalty in cases of apostasy (articles 96 and 167–72).

A further example comes from the penal law of Mauritania of 1984: article 306 states that "all Muslims guilty of apostasy, both in words and in action, in an evident way, will be invited to repent for a period of three days. If in this period of time he does not repent, he is condemned to death as an apostate, and his possessions will be confiscated in favor of the treasury."

Other countries punish apostasy with severe penalties, but they do not resort to the death penalty.

60.   *What are the most famous cases of condemnations pronounced toward apostates?*

The *fatwā* issued by Ayatollah Khomeini in 1989 condemning author Salman Rushdie to death for authoring *The Satanic Verses* is the best-known episode. The incident clearly demonstrated and presented, on the world level, the problem Muslims have in dealing with the issue of apostasy well outside the borders of the Islamic community.

I distinctly remember the 1995 condemnation of university professor Naṣr Ḥāmid Abū Zayd, whom we have already discussed,[30] and the case of the writer Nawāl al-Saʿdāwī, who in 2001 was brought to court by a Muslim lawyer and charged with apostasy despite the protests of many feminist organizations and associations for the defense of human rights. These intellectuals were able to escape punishment only because of global interest in their cases.

[30] See question 42, p. 98 above.

Less fortunate was the Egyptian intellectual Farag Foda, assassinated in June 1992 by a radical commando shortly after he was declared an apostate by the religious authorities. During the trial of Foda's murderers, sheikh Muḥammad al-Ghazāli, well known for his moderation, witnessed in favor of the defense and justified the assassination of Foda based on the *sharīᶜa*.

In 1995 an assassin targeted the 83-year-old Egyptian writer Naguib Maḥfouz, the first Arab to be awarded the Nobel Prize for Literature (1988). His name is associated with many literary works and films. It was his novel *Children of the Alley*, written in the 1950s and still banished in Egypt, where it is considered blasphemous by many, that was the cause of the failed assassination attempt.

The Bengalese writer Taslima Nasreen was obliged to live in hiding because of the threats by fundamentalist groups who asked that she be arrested and put to death for blasphemy. In 1994, Taslima Nasreen was accused of an "offense against religion", a crime provided for in the penal code of Bangladesh, and she was obliged to seek refuge in the West.

Many cases are far less known by the non-Muslim world. These generally involve common people. One of these is Muhammad Omer Haji, a twenty-seven-year-old Somali refugee living in Yemen, who despite his refugee status was sentenced to death in 2000 because he had converted to Christianity along with his wife. In prison, he was tortured in order to convince him to reveal the names of his "accomplices" and abjure his faith. When no confession or revelation of names was forthcoming, the judge gave Haji one week to declare, three times, his formal return to Islam under the pain of death. The intervention of some international organizations allowed him to escape the punishment. He now lives, together with his family, in New Zealand, where he enjoys a sort of "religious" asylum.

In 1994, four Muslims, who twenty years earlier had converted to Christianity and later became catechists in the Sudanese diocese of Rumbeck, were not so fortunate: they were beaten by the government security forces and then crucified because they refused to return to Islam.

It is well known as well that the Saudi government condemned many Shiites to death under the accusation of apostasy in order to get rid of troublesome political adversaries. The Saudi *ulemā* provided the theological foundation for this measure by issuing some *fatwā* in which they declared the Shiites to be "polytheists" since "they pray to Ali[31] in moments of difficulty and discouragement" and asked Muslims not to marry them and not to buy meat butchered by them.[32]

In 2006, the now well-known citizen of Afghanistan Abdul Rahman was arrested on a charge of apostasy from Islam. His trial attracted international attention and indignation. Largely because of international pressure, Abdul Rahman escaped the death penalty because of "mental incompetence". He now lives in Italy, where he was granted asylum.

61.   *What is the current status of the debate on apostasy in the Islamic world?*

Any debate discussion is usually limited to very narrow circles of intellectuals and to experts in law. Recently the discussion started to expand into the public forum and to become the object of discussion in the mass media, which shows the level of importance given to this problem in Muslim societies.

[31] Ali bin Abī Ṭālib, Muhammad's cousin and son-in-law. Apart from being the fourth khalif, he is the first *imām* for the Shiites.

[32] For the cases of the beheading of "apostate" Shiites, see Amnesty International's *Saudi Arabia, Religious Intolerance: The Arrest, Detention and Torture of Christian Worshippers and Shi'a Muslims*, published in 1993.

The stakes, on the level of principles, are very high: behind specific cases, there is the problem of freedom of conscience. If one goes to the root of the issue, one finds a fundamental question at stake, namely: Is an Islam in which religion and state are separated conceivable?

The condemnation of apostasy is presently justified from an appeal to observe a very literal traditionalist interpretation of both the Qur'ān and of the *sunna*. This has been reintroduced and encouraged by the fundamentalists. With a series of logical connections, the traditionalists can draw the conclusion that calling apostasy into question means doubting the absolute value of the Qur'ān. Therefore, criticizing the *ḥadd* (canonical punishment),[33] derived from sacred text, in the name of modernity means undermining the whole traditionalist structure and declaring that the Qur'ān is no longer a literal reference point for modern Muslims and non-Muslims alike.[34]

D. A Provocation: Reciprocity

62. *In many countries with a Muslim majority population, there are still many limits on an authentic religious freedom, especially for Christians. Presently, in Europe, where the Muslim communities are multiplying, their requests to exercise publicly their faith are increasing. There are those who demand the application of the so-called principle of reciprocity, that is, translating the religious opportunities that have been allowed in the West toward Muslims*

[33] See question 45, p. 103 above.

[34] For more on the subject of apostasy, see Samir Khalil Samir's article in "Le débat autour du délit d'apostasie dans l'Islam contemporain" [The Debate on the Crime of Apostasy in Contemporary Islam], in *Faith, Power and Violence*, ed. John Donohue and Christian Troll, Orientalia Christiana Analecta 258 (Rome: Pontificio Istituto Orientale, 1998), 115–40.

(for instance, erecting places of worship) to analogous measures that should be granted to Christians living in Islamic countries. What do you think about this?

This is a burning issue that divides even Christians, who seem to be the most interested in the application of the principle of reciprocity. However, I believe that even in this case, one must first clear the field of a basic and deep-seated misunderstanding: we are not talking about a "religious" problem. What is really at stake is the possibility of people exercising their human rights, of which the religious ones are an important and vital component. Therefore, reciprocity is not just doing a favor for Christians but realizing justice for all people independent from their religious faith. For this purpose, the commitment of the international community is necessary.

In recent times, on many occasions, there has been international political, diplomatic, and economic pressure applied in order to oblige a country to modify its behavior or to protect human rights that have been violated. One need think only of the American embargoes against Cuba and Gaddafi's Libya (the latter after the Lockerbie terrorist attack) or the embargo approved by the United Nations against Iraq after the invasion of Kuwait (with serious consequences for the population rather than for Saddam Hussein). I also remember the pressures applied by Europe, with Italy in the lead, on the Turkish government to stop the execution of the PKK (Kurdistan Worker's Party) leader Abdullah Ocalan. The European Union is applying pressure on the Turkish city of Ankara to modify its laws and behavior in the field of human rights, for instance, by abolishing the death penalty and recognizing the rights of the Kurdish population. There are also campaigns to raise awareness and apply pressure on governments in order to end the practice of genital mutilation of women, still largely practiced in many countries.

Taking all of this into consideration, the immense and absurd silence and the absence of diplomatic efforts by international organizations with regard to religious freedom is perturbing. It is as if the religious aspect is marginal and irrelevant.

63.   *What are the reasons for this void, this general lack of Western government action for religious freedom in Muslim nations? Why does the defense of religious freedom seem to be of so little interest for Europe and the West?*

There are two primary reasons. The first is connected to the importance of economic relations between the West and certain Islamic countries, primarily Saudi Arabia and the Arab Emirates but also some others less rich and powerful though still very meaningful on the chessboard of economic interests. Evidently, it is more difficult to raise one's voice, protest, or make requests when millions of dollars of business are involved. We raised our voices (rightly) against the violations perpetrated in the Balkans by Serbia, but we remain silent on the violations of human rights in Saudi Arabia, well aware that in the second case, we risk the profits connected with oil.

The West has great respect for human rights but even greater respect for material advantages and wealth. If there is some conflict related to economic or commercial interests, human rights are placed second. If the defense of human rights implies the sacrifice of economic advantages, the rights are normally sacrificed, not the economic advantages.

The second reason for the inertia is closely connected to the first one. The European countries, which are more and more influenced by modern, secular culture, consider religious freedom a minor issue. They appear to believe that religion is something of the historical past, old-fashioned, and a source of problems and divisions that should be abandoned at the lowest levels of international diplomacy.

64. *Concretely, what ought to be done? What strategies could be followed? Is reciprocity doomed to remain a flag periodically waved by some "insurmountable" people, or can it become a theme upon which we can progress and reach tangible results?*

A good opportunity for the West to raise the matter of reciprocity with a Muslim nation comes from what is happening to immigrating Muslims, who are increasingly asking to build mosques and centers for the diffusion of Islam in Europe. Well, why not set as a condition of their practicing religious freedom openly in the West that the same religious expressions that they rightly demand must also be granted to non-Muslim believers in their countries of origin?

Moreover, the provision of aid for the development of some countries could easily be accompanied (and conditioned) by the demand that non-Muslims be granted permission to build places of worship or even be granted freedom of religious expression by their Muslim country of residence. It would be a sort of *sine qua non* condition that characterizes economic cooperation but is established for a greater goal, namely, increased freedom for all people.

To those who object that this would mean giving up the tradition of tolerance and freedom that characterizes the West, I would like to say that it is in the name of this tradition that economic embargoes as well as diplomatic and political pressures were applied. Ought this to be done for such a serious matter as religious freedom?

65. *If the Western nations were to make authorization for the construction of mosques within their national borders conditional*

on similar measures that should be taken in Islamic countries in favor of Christians, we penalize Muslim immigrants by unjustly considering them responsible for the limits imposed on religious freedom in their native countries by their rulers. Do you not think this is a wrong approach to solving the problem?

I am not talking about individual immigrants; that would be silly. Let us not forget that the leaders of the countries that are most often accused of setting the limitations on religious freedom refuse to deal with the problem by claiming that nothing can change because "the problem is the population" and that changing some laws or some habits would be a dangerous venture because it would clash against a centuries-old mentality.

Here is a significant episode: in the 1980s, when President Anwar al-Sādāt appointed the Christian Boutros Boutros-Ghali to serve as Egypt's minister of foreign affairs, there were days of riots and protests (fueled by individuals and groups connected to the powerful Muslim university of al-Azhar) that finally obliged the president to withdraw the appointment. At the time, it was said: "See. People do not accept a countercurrent choice like that of entrusting foreign politics to a non-Muslim; therefore, one cannot pass over co-citizens [that is, Muslims] for appointments."

As for reciprocity, I maintain that in order to avoid this shifting of responsibility from the rulers to the population, one must work on two fronts: first, by applying diplomatic, political, and economic pressure (as in setting conditions for receiving foreign aid) on the governments that impede the exercise of religious freedom; second, by asking immigrating Muslims and their organizations, which are active and ever ready to protest in order to claim their rights in the West, to work in the same manner toward achieving similar rights for non-Muslims from the authorities of their native countries.

It is evident that in both cases there is a preliminary condition for whatever request is made. Much stronger attention must be paid to the issue of religious rights and freedom by international organizations and the authorities of each country. All of this in turn demands the mobilization of society and religious institutions.

Lastly, it is necessary to remember that the nations who financially support the actual construction of most of the mosques in the world are Saudi Arabia and some Gulf nations. These are the very same states that forbid the construction of any non-Muslim religious structures and strongly limit religious freedom. In my opinion, this money should be considered "dirty" money, as is done with the funds that sustain terrorism. Suitable measures could be taken in order to block its use in Europe or at least to tie its usage to the establishment of a greater religious freedom in Saudi Arabia and the Gulf states. The request must come from the Western governments in order to achieve some form of religious reciprocity for non-Muslim populations living in Muslim nations. The essential request from the European governments is required for a minimum of coherence. It is their credibility that is at stake! However, they need some courage: will they be capable of demonstrating it?

IV. Islam among Us

A. European Islam or Islamized Europe?

66.   *After the attack on the World Trade Center "Twin Tow-*
ers" buildings in New York City on September 11, 2001, it
became apparent that a network of organizations, with many dif-
ferent strategies, had settled in various European countries. They
were preparing violent attacks and enlisting people ready to accom-
plish them. Do you think that these are radical groups isolated
from the larger Muslim communities, or are they a project of global
Islamization that was announced long ago but was often ignored
or minimized?

I believe that the discovery of logistic and operational bases
for the preparation of attacks as well as the detection of
people accused of belonging to terrorist groups in various
European countries shed a sinister light and bring us up-to-
date on what I call the current "violent" phase of Islamic
expansion.

With respect to the international Islamic community, Muslims in the countries of the European Union number only
twelve million adherents. From a numerical point of view,
this is a very limited group. Some members may plan clandestine activity, and it is detached from the most significant
Islamic organizations. Contacts with the organizations are
not completely absent because of attendance at certain
mosques and Islamic centers, especially in big cities. Many

of these activists theorize about resorting to the use of force to affirm Islam in the whole world. These individuals appeal to *jihād* in its violent meaning.[1]

In recent years, these groups operated in Europe, sometimes conducting military actions or leading demonstrations. By way of example, I distinctly recall some episodes attributed to the Algerian GIA (Armed Islamic Group): a bomb exploded on February 3, 1986, in the Champs Elysées (three hours later, another bomb was defused on the third floor of the Eiffel Tower); on March 20, 1986, another explosion occurred in the Point Show Gallery in Paris, leaving 2 dead and 29 injured; an explosion in the subway of the French capital on July 25, 1995, killed 7 people and wounded another 117. The police in different European countries, but especially Italy, have long been investigating many plots for attacks that were organized but never carried out. The investigators have discovered logistic bases in different cities that were used to host the activists of "fighting groups" in transit to other countries or were related to terrorist organizations such as al-Qāʿida and the Algeria-based Salafiyyah Group for Preaching and Combat (GSPC).

It is correct, therefore, to talk of a real network that over the years has expanded into different European countries. This network has justifiably aroused worries because a limited number of fighters is sufficient to terrorize an entire country, as we see in Palestine, Algeria, Indonesia, and the Mindanao region in the Philippines. One must not forget that the radical groups that form the breeding ground of these clandestine organizations are growing strong and increasing their influence as well as their enlistment capacity within the Muslim "base".

---

[1] See chapter 2, section C, pp. 62–80 above.

67.   *Some observers claim that, for a long time, the strength of*
the religious and cultural roots and the control exercised by the
native countries will remain an influential force in the immigrant
communities in Europe. This will constitute an obstacle for the real
integration and the creation of a "European" Islam. Allow me to
use a concise but telling sentence: Instead of a Westernization of
Islam, the risk is the Islamization of the West. There are even
those who denounce the danger of an Islamic "invasion" as a trend
that, acting at the cultural and religious level, would also make use
of the migratory currents as instruments for the propagation and
the affirmation of Islam. Are these alarmist fears or well-grounded
concerns?

First of all, one must bear in mind the nature of Islam. As
we have already seen, Islam since its origin has affirmed
itself as a universal message and project; namely, it has
affirmed that Islam is good for all people and that the whole
world is created to accept its proposal. How can the project
of worldwide conversion, already announced in the Qur'ān,
be achieved? Historically, three tendencies have developed:
the most extreme (about which we have already talked) con-
templates the recourse to violence and to military action.
In recent times, this method has increased in popularity.

The second trend is what we could define as "mystical-
spiritual". It has as its goal the Muslim return to the lost
authenticity of Islam and the propagation of the message
of the Qur'ān among non-Muslim populations. Muslims
depend on the thirst for sacredness that exists within many
individuals in modern society, even though it is mostly dis-
regarded by commentators. The Muslim "offering" of transcendental answers finds a fertile soil in Europe among
atheists and agnostics as well as among many Christians
who have been disappointed by the behavior of their church
leaders, who seem less and less capable of dealing with

basic human and spiritual needs. By way of this same perspective, one can readily understand the spread of Buddhism, the New Age movement, and other spiritual and religious phenomena in Western societies.

The third tendency, which we could describe as sociopolitical, intends to Islamize society as the premise for a growing political influence and for the eventual institution of Islamic governments. As we saw before, this tendency originates in Islamic countries but is also applied in many different contexts. When Muslim migration turned toward European countries, the strategists of the radical movements developed the theory of the Islamization of the Old Continent, which was expressed in books and *fatāwi* issued on different occasions. This was part of a global plan devoted to the creation of a world dominated by Islam. This goal will ultimately be reached after many years (perhaps centuries will be needed), but it is considered an inevitable movement of history.

I offer three examples to help people understand the dynamics of the Islamization process currently afoot in the West.

Some time ago, the Lebanese Shiite sheikh Muḥammad Ḥussein Faḍlallah, an authoritative Muslim representative, spoke on Beirut television during a meeting with some Christian representatives. He asserted that the European democratic system represents the best opportunity for the propagation of Islam on the Continent. He described it as the channel for the easiest spreading of the messenger's message.

The second example comes from Abdul-Hadi Palazzi, spokesman for AMI, the Associazione Musulmani Italiani (the Italian Muslim Association), one of the Islamic organizations that sent a representative of the Islamic community, with regard to the organization's candidacy, to the negotiations to reach an agreement with the Italian government.[2] He claims that, along with the migration of Muslims from North Africa and Asia toward the end of the 1970s in Italy and Europe,

> there is an international political project launched by the Muslim Brotherhood, ... an extremist movement that, behind a pseudo-religious façade, hides its goal to create a controlling network capable of conditioning from inside the life of Islamic countries, exploiting religious sentiments toward a political radicalization. This organization has decided to extend its influence also to the communities of immigrants in western Europe. For this purpose, many activists are sent to Europe on scholarships to study, officially to obtain a degree, but in reality to establish the bases of the Muslim Brotherhood. For Italy the operational center is the University for Foreigners in Perugia, and in this city the Union of Muslim Students in Italy (USMI), the name under which the Muslim Brotherhood operated in the beginning, was founded.

Palazzi asserts that in the following years, with the support of enormous amounts of financial aid coming from abroad, a network of Islamic centers in different cities was created. This was the preliminary step toward what in the 1990s would become the Union of Islamic Communities and Organizations in Italy (UCOII), another association that is trying to negotiate an agreement with the Italian government.[3]

The third example comes from Archbishop Giuseppe Bernardini of Izmir, Turkey, who on the occasion of the European synod held in Rome in October 1999 reported the declarations that an authoritative Muslim representative

---

[2] See appendix C, "Islam in Italy".

[3] For a wider illustration, cf. Silvio Ferrari, ed., *L'Islam in Europa: Lo statuto giuridico delle comunità musulmane* [Islam in Europe: The Juridical Status of Muslim Communities] (Bologna: Il Mulino, 1996), 296–303.

released during an official Islamic-Christian meeting: "Thanks to your democratic laws, we shall invade you. Thanks to our religious laws, we shall dominate you." Bernardini himself insisted that oil revenues accrued by Saudi Arabia and other Islamic countries "are not used to create new jobs in the poor countries of North Africa and the Middle East but to build mosques and cultural centers in the Christian countries with Islamic immigration, Rome included. How can we not see in all this a clear program of expansion and reconquest?"[4]

68.   *Mosques, Islamic centers, and qur'ānic schools are multiplying in Europe. So also are the loudspeakers and sound systems that call Muslims to prayer. In their neighborhoods, Muslims maintain distinct ways of dressing and say their collective prayers in the streets and public squares. What does all this very public Muslim activity symbolize? It is becoming more and more widespread throughout Europe?*

All the public activity expresses a strong Muslim desire to assert the Islamic presence in the public arena, out of all private and family environments. It represents the same logic of Islamization that I have just described. I have no intention of nurturing alarmism, but based on my knowledge of the history of Islam and on my personal experiences in numerous Muslim countries, I would like to highlight some issues that may not be noticed by Westerners but are very significant.

Consider the importance given by Muslims to outward appearance: dressing in a certain way, wearing the *ḥijāb*, and having a long beard are much more than fashion (as we

would think in Europe) or the respect for some tradition
(as it is for some African and Asian populations). These are
the visible means to emphasize an identity that is at the
same time religious, cultural, and social. In Muslim countries, very real political disputes between those with liberal
beliefs on the one side and followers of extremist and radical currents on the other side have developed around these
public image issues.

During the 1980s, the Egyptian government prohibited
males from growing a beard because it was considered a
typical symbol of the Muslim Brotherhood organization.
During Nasser's presidency (1952–1970), many posters were
seen on the streets of Egyptian cities with the statement
"Popular clothing is better than the *jallābiyya* [the traditional clothing of peasants]." Nasser was clearly conscious
of how important it was to suppress the garment in order
to overcome the peasant mentality and encourage openness
to modernity. Starting from that premise, he organized a
campaign to mold public opinion and limit the influence
of the radical movements, which had made the wearing of
a certain type of garment the mark that expressed the claims
to Muslim tradition.

The most significant and obvious of all symbolic elements is the mosque with a dome and minaret, outfitted
with loudspeakers and other amplification instruments for
announcing the call to prayer as extensively and pervasively
as possible. It is a very simple way of pursuing the Islamization of the whole space by means of auditory and visual
signs.[5]

Each day, collective prayers are said in the squares and on
sidewalks by Muslims. There are very public manifestations

---

[5] For the problems connected with the mosque, see section D, "The
Mosque: A Muslim Church?" questions 86–88, pp. 167–72 below.

of religious belief on the occasions of feasts such as Eid al-Fitr ('Īd al-Fiṭr), which marks the end of the Ramaḍān fasting, that visibly highlight the Muslim presence in a city. It asserts the existence of a new protagonist on the public scene with qualities of radical otherness and nonconformity. However, I notice that the common, secularized, and disenchanted Western citizen considers all this as merely folkloric color. Westerners regard it as one of the many characteristics of a multicultural society and do not grasp its highly evocative significance. When many Muslims prostrate themselves in prayer on a Friday in Duomo Square in Milan, as has happened, they symbolically take possession of the most important square of the city. I am surprised that Westerners do not appreciate the sociopolitical dimension of all this. It would be sufficient for authorities to apply the laws equally for everybody. The city streets and public square are civic places, and nobody should occupy them for religious events if they do not have special permits to hold such gatherings for a specific circumstance. This principle should be applicable to both Friday prayers for Muslims as well as for Catholic processions.

69.   *One of the most controversial Muslim symbols is the traditional veil (hijāb) worn by young women. It has long been a cause of controversy, especially in French schools, where many principals have prohibited it because they considered the veil a display of the Muslims' otherness and of their refusal to integrate into French society. Can you suggest any solution to this problem?*

In order to understand what is taking place, we must start from what happens in many Muslim countries, where the veil is a symbol that for a long time has been used by the radical movements to symbolize an alternative position for

Muslims with respect to the secular governments. It became the instrumental means for achieving political goals in Muslim countries. It is not by chance that some governments in secularized nations like Syria, Tunisia, and Turkey have expressively forbidden wearing the veil in schools and in public offices in order to slow the escalation of radical movements. However, Europeans must recognize that many young Muslim women wear the veil as an expression of personal religious conviction, even though this is sometimes done under the influence of adults (parents or an *imām*).

The result of this double reality is the ambiguity of the symbol, and this explains the difficulty of managing the problem in a pluralistic context like Europe. Therefore, it is the duty of the people in charge of the environments where the problem arises to consider the concrete circumstances they face, to evaluate the real intentions of those involved, and to base their decisions on the particular girls and their families. This is an issue that can be solved through a reasonable and purposeful dialogue more than through general measures that do not take into account all the different circumstances.

70. *In light of the aforesaid considerations, can we say that a sort of "long march" of Islam in European societies is developing?*

From the Muslim communities, there are different signs, which show diverse approaches. There are those who plan a penetration of Europe that uses the instruments of Western democracies, such as pluralism and freedom of expression. Yet there are also those Muslims who practice their faith privately and participate in its public manifestations without the goal of a religious, social, or political expansion of Islam.

What is happening among young people is very interesting. By the second or third generation of immigrants, there are those Muslims who have developed a position that reconciles the values of the West with those of their Muslim identity. They exhibit different behaviors from those practiced in their countries of origin or by their parents (or grandparents) of the first generation. Many young Moroccans are proud of being French citizens and Muslims and are able to elaborate a personal synthesis between Islam and secular society.

In evaluating the possibility of a "silent Islamization" of Europe, one must not underestimate the fact that emigration, especially that of young Muslims, is a sort of safety valve that allows governments in the developing countries to mitigate the widespread social tensions deriving from high unemployment rates, from poverty and anxiety over lack of opportunity in the population. The immigration of hundreds of thousands of "unsatisfied" people into Europe from nations along the southern coast of the Mediterranean may reproduce the same social tensions in Europe as in their homeland. Immigrants are always the first to suffer from economic downturns and employment crises. Among the immigrating Muslims, largely due to the influence of propaganda created by the radical organizations, is the very strong conviction that a return to a rigorous practice of Islam is the only true solution to their difficulties. This makes the immigrants more susceptible to the appeals of those who cultivate the dream of the Islamization of society, even in old Europe in places where religious convictions and cultural references are less solid, for that presents territory where a smooth expansion is possible.

European countries cannot simply renounce the principles of democracy, pluralism, and freedom that characterize their juridical and legislative systems out of the fear of a cultural and religious invasion by Muslims. Freedom of worship and of social expression can be accorded to Muslims, provided that their requests made in the name of the Muslim faith are not accompanied by claims to change the rules of civil life.

However, it would be shortsighted to limit ourselves to a defensive attitude. For Europeans, both the immigration and the growth of Muslim communities represent a historical challenge. This is an event that in the Christian terms may be defined as "providential". In fact, this new situation obliges Europeans to examine in depth what gives substance to their societies as well as the models for possible coexistence, and the rules that must govern it.

71.   *Approximately twelve million Muslims live in the countries of the European Union. Some of these Muslims even hold citizenship in the country where they are living. It is therefore inaccurate to identify them as immigrants or as Moroccans, Algerians, Tunisians, or Turks since they are citizens. Slowly, but inexorably, the DNA of the Old Continent is transforming. Europe is fast becoming more multicultural and multireligious. What dynamics can be expected in the further construction of modern Europe, given the presence of all these new inhabitants asking for citizenship and rights?*

It is certainly correct to acknowledge the present transformations. However, it is necessary to clarify certain reference points; otherwise one risks being overcome by emotions and perhaps by the political opportunities of the present moment.

First, let us not forget the simple fact that the twelve million Muslims represent only 3 percent of the total resident European population and that the Muslims who hold citizenship in their countries of residence are still a minority in the total population of those nations. But they are a very visible minority. This fact is often amplified and emphasized by the mass media. In Italy, for instance, Italian citizens of Muslim faith number in the thousands but represent less than 0.1 percent of the total Italian population.

We must ask who comprises the majority population in any nation, and what holds that majority together? Only then can we know on what foundation the new Europe is being constructed.

Although it may not be considered politically correct, history teaches us that the roots of the European civilization are almost exclusively Christian. It is Christianity itself that in the course of the centuries was able to combine with other cultural and religious traditions to give life to a pluralistic civilization. So, despite its pluralistic nature, Europe is not some indefinite entity. Europe has a Christian foundation and core values.

This means that when one talks about a multireligious Europe, one cannot think of making a clean sweep of centuries of history. The new cultural and religious groups that arrive on the Continent must harmonize themselves in the house already established. They must enter the common house that is being renovated and not demand to have a separate one built expressly for them. The thesis expounded by some Muslim representatives (for example, Ṭāriq Ramaḍān, the nephew of Ḥassan al-Bannā, who was founder of the Muslim Brotherhood) is that Europe is multireligious and that Christians must be aware that they are no longer the majority. I think that this point of view is doubly wrong, first at the statistical level and then at the cultural one. Any agnostic Italian is as *culturally* Christian as I, an Arab Christian, am *culturally* Muslim. In other words, even if Italians in general are no longer practicing Christians, the majority will declare or perceive themselves as being Christian in faith.

72.   *During the difficult construction of the European Union, all discussion of the economic-financial and political-institutional*

aspects has generally ignored any considerations of topics connected with "foundations". In the Charter of Fundamental Rights of the European Union, approved in Nice, France, in December 2000, all references to the religious roots of the Continent were discarded and a more generic formulation was chosen, which was limited to remembering the "spiritual and moral heritage" of the European peoples. Now that the representatives of the different countries of the [European] Convention are dealing with the drafting of the first European constitution, the basic questions concerning Europe's historical foundations are emerging again, but the Christian tradition seems doomed to play the role of Cinderella by being there but ignored and forgotten.

I have the impression that for the sake of pursuing modernity, Europeans are at risk of losing their historical memory. For those who study history with intellectual honesty, as well as those observers of individual and collective behaviors, it is clear that the values and ideals that characterize the European continent are nearly impossible to explain without reconnecting them to the Christian tradition, which, assimilated with the Greco-Roman and the Jewish traditions, constitutes Europe's foundation. When I, a Christian Arab permeated with Muslim culture, discovered the Europe of the 1950s and particularly the Italy of the 1970s, I realized how incomprehensible this civilization was without reference to the Christian tradition. And the changes that occurred later in the habits of these countries did not cancel this footprint, which is rooted in centuries of history.

Even the values that for a long time were contrasted with that tradition, such as tolerance and freedom of thought—that is, the rights proclaimed in the secular institutions of the West—are not fully comprehensible without referring to their Judeo-Christian origins. And, despite the efforts of some secular thinkers who claim the exclusive paternity of freedom and maintain that there is absolute disparity between personal freedom and religious thought, the contribution of Christianity remains a decisive factor.

It is not by accident that the secular idea for the separation of church and state, the separation of faith and politics, developed in the West and seems inconceivable in the Muslim world. It is no accident that the clearest formulation of human rights was born in the West and now encounters difficulties in expanding into the Muslim world. The fundamental reason for all this is the Christian inspiration of Western civilization that, over the centuries, was capable of integrating also the secular values of Hellenism and of other cultures.

In secular France, when one speaks of Muslims, they are considered a radically different component of society apart from the Christian culture on which the nation was founded. Formally, and in the name of secularism, the sociocultural dimension of Christianity is denied by the French; however, when dealing with Muslims, they cannot avoid considering them the "others". But "other" as compared to what, if not to what historically constitutes the foundation of that transalpine nation that has such strong roots in Christianity?

The risk that I see is that the European Union will give itself a constitution without a soul. Hence it will be a building with fragile foundations, a giant with feet of clay.

B. The Role of Converts

73. *Inside the Muslim community in Europe, there is a numerically insignificant minority who enjoy a certain visibility, especially in the mass media. These are the European converts to Islam.*

What in your opinion are the reasons that lead a European to approach the Qur'ān?

Each conversion belongs to the mystery of each person's freedom, and any attempt to explain it is approximate. However, one can make some general observations.

In Europe, there exists a widespread interest in strong existential positions that are more appealing than living a watered-down version of Christianity. For many people in search of meaning in life, Christianity seems made up of halfway compromises, doubts, and fears, too many "perhaps" and "I do not knows" than convictions and certainties. Islam conveys security, a sense of belonging, and proposes a series of laws that regulate the whole of a believer's life. Muslims know in what way one must pray, behave, and eat. There are those who can be easily attracted by a life regulated according to precise rules. Such a life seems a reassuring refuge from the widespread relativism of European culture.

One particular category of converts is those who approach Islam for reasons of marriage. A Muslim woman cannot marry a man of another faith. From the Muslim religious point of view, prior conversion of the future husband, which must be certified by an Islamic authority, is necessary for the marriage to be valid. There are also some women who convert to Islam before, or after, marrying a Muslim male.

Other people are charmed by Islam during a journey abroad, by spiritual readings, or by developing a friendship with some Muslim immigrant living in Europe. Some individuals decide to convert because they are disenchanted with politics; many of these are former militants, who often have years of experience in groups of the extreme left or right and who revise their civil involvement in the light of the cultural categories of Islam. They identify with Islam as an alternative system in which their motivations to assist oppressed people in their struggle against neocolonialism, to resist consumerism and Western values, and to resist what is considered the Western religion par excellence, Christianity, are sublimated.

Apart from the conversions to Islam connected to the so-called marriage obligations, the most powerful impulse for conversion is substantially the strong mystical and spiritual dimension of man, which leads to the search for the sacred. This is a very widespread phenomenon now in European societies. Islam has the appeal of a religion with a strong all-absorbing drive that displays itself on the public scene with no inferiority complex and claims a way of life that requires social visibility.

The convert's imagination tends to make an association between the West and its weakened culture and Islam with its strong culture. In an increasingly secular society, people are fascinated by the claim that the religious element is an integral part of the individual and the community, by the call of a religion that does not pursue people by supporting and justifying their weaknesses. Rather, by presenting itself as a global and pervasive alternative, Islam depicts itself and is perceived as an integrated and compelling way of life. It is like a dish with strong flavors when compared to the "tasteless soups" normally served on Western tables. Ultimately, it is seen by the convert as a convincing answer to a search for meaning that was left unanswered by watered-down Christianity.

Finally, we must not forget that the very possibility of adhering to a different religion and of professing it in public is granted by the free environment that developed in Europe, thanks to the Christian vision of the human being and of society. A similar situation is practically impossible to achieve or at least very difficult to find in Islamic countries because of the general intolerance of Muslims toward others.

74. *Can the European convert act as a bridge between Muslim immigrants and the countries that receive them?*

I am skeptical about this hypothesis, although it is fascinating for the possibilities it offers. As a matter of fact, the converts enjoy many advantages. They speak the language of the country in which they live, and they know the traditions, habits, and mentality of the population. However, over the years, having known many such converts, I have found that, generally (apart from some significant exceptions), they have a limited knowledge of Islam and of its traditions, or they have an idea of Islam that does not correspond much to reality.

Moreover, based on my personal experiences in several countries, I must say that, unfortunately, many of the converts do not stand out for their commitment toward a real integration of Muslims with Westerners. On the contrary, they tend to underline the irreconcilable differences between Islam and the host country. This position, perhaps, is influenced by the fact that their encounter with Islam arrived after an intellectual or spiritual quest marked by personal rejection of Western values.

Many converts assume radical positions (and this happens in all religions), perhaps to justify to themselves their change of direction. Strong equilibrium is needed for one successfully to change his lifestyle and religious belief. A convert needs to be balanced in order to integrate both the person he was and the person he has become. Certainly the majority of Muslim immigrants have as their primary goal a decent life for themselves and their families, and they have neither time nor the inclination to deal with politics. Converts, however, often make the sociopolitical arena their battle horse and will fight in order to obtain a particular statute or some exceptions to general rules and in the process become the spokespersons of the whole community. Some converts, by their manner of dress or the behavior they adopt, stand out as having an "exotic" attitude that emphasizes their difference from mainstream society, while immigrants, in general, tend to maintain a low profile or in any case do not dress and act in such a way as to be readily identified as Muslims. In short, converts often seem to strive to be more Muslim than the Muslims.

75. *Do you think that young people, the second- and third-generation descendants of immigrants, are the protagonists of a desirable process of integration of Islam in the European societies?*

Every instance of immigration is an occasion to meet diversity, and it therefore offers opportunities for exchange, for reciprocal enrichment, resulting in changes that can be set in motion especially by those who arrive but also by the societies who receive them.

If one takes a superficial look, one would agree that those who were born in a foreign land, or those who spent their childhood and adolescence there during the time their personality was being formed, have the instruments to understand better the mechanisms and values that regulate coexistence. They can appreciate their adopted country's advantages as compared to those available in their ancestral homeland. Quite often the young people become the spokespersons for a less conflicted relationship than what characterized the first-generation immigrants.

Young people everywhere have a strong desire for identification with friends of the same age. They are prompted to assimilate and acquire the attitudes, trends, and values of their friends to avoid feeling excluded. They want to become "one of them". If there is a conflict between the values of tradition and the values encountered in school or in the group of friends, it is very likely that the latter will prevail over the former. This is especially evident among Muslim girls, for whom contrasts are more evident and stronger. All of this alters the way in which one perceives and expresses one's own cultural and religious identity. Some conflicts may also arise in the immigrant family that normally tends to remain tied to traditional values. Such generational conflicts have become the object of books, films, theater plays, and songs. All this has convinced some analysts to infer that the young Muslims represent the new frontier of a gradual movement toward a European Islam that is more open to the values of secularism and modernity.

However, a careful analysis of the current situation allows us to see a very different process. I am referring, for instance, to what happens in some Parisian *banlieues* or in the Arab-Muslim neighborhoods of other large European cities. There the young immigrants are the protagonists of what is called "the return to Islam", that is, an appropriation, assimilation, and application of their own religiously rooted radical and anti-Western positions against any form of integration into European society. It is based on strict discipline and intransigence. It interprets religious belonging as a conflict. They aim for Muslim superimposition on the society in which they live more than toward any integration with it. And in these matters, it is often the children who accuse their parents of betraying their original Muslim heritage and of having moved away from true Islam. This conflict within the Muslim community is sometimes fueled by the radical organizations that try to push young people toward positions that are far from integration and toward everything that tends to be in opposition to the West.

76.   *What elements do you think might encourage a process of integration of Islam into Europe?*

I believe that coexistence within a society must be based on fundamental principles such as the respect of human rights, the equality between men and women, democracy and pluralism, religious freedom, and separation between religion and state. In the long run, these may positively influence the Islamic communities. However, this is not an automatic process, and to promote it, some conditions are required.

1. The government authorities must support the aforementioned principles, which allowed Europe to become a lighthouse of civilization and a land of welcome and freedom. Also, governments must be willing to accept that form of Islam that is not at odds with the juridical and legislative organization of Western countries and their integrated practice in other countries. A very significant discussion of this matter recently took place in Great Britain. The British home secretary proposed a campaign to encourage integration among the different foreign communities. Immigrants were encouraged to adopt British rules of behavior. The secretary stated, "We cannot tolerate the intolerable just because it is masked as a cultural difference." He warned against the potential explosion of conflicts that British society already knew from its long experience as a land of immigration. The conflicts usually grow out of the fact that some foreign community representatives insist on declaring themselves British and simultaneously claim the right to retain habits and practices connected to their traditional cultures.[6]

---

[6] About this, see "Immigrati, la sfida inglese: Un test per vivere da noi" [Immigrants, the English Challenge: A Test to Live Here], *La Repubblica*, December 10, 2001.

Significant as well is the German controversy over the so-called *Leitkultur*, the reference culture, for all those who live in Germany. It is interesting to notice that the word *Leitkultur* was coined by Bassam Tibi, a German political scientist of Syrian origin and of Muslim faith who declares himself "in favor of cultural diversity but firmly against multiculturalism". He opposed the attempts of the radical Muslim organizations that, "in the name of the rights of the community and of the right to the preservation of the cultural identity, demand that *sharīᶜa* be applied to Muslim immigrants in Germany." As a liberal Muslim, he opposed this position because "*sharīᶜa* would collide with the secularism prevailing in Europe and would be against the European constitutions."[7]

2. It is necessary for the desire of Muslim immigrants to become full citizens of the societies that receive them to grow, without any ambiguity or nostalgia for the past. There can be no pretense that only the introduction of Muslim juridical models, in force in their countries of origin, can allow the full expression of the immigrants' religious faith. On the contrary, religious freedom for all people is already granted by the constitutions of the European countries.

3. Lastly, at an elementary level, in daily life, the process of school integration can play a fundamental role in the dynamics of cultural integration, leading to the insertion of Muslim women into the working world. This can augment the process of female emancipation from a situation of inferiority and submission. Day-to-day relations with neighbors, coexistence in the workplace, and whatever encourages reciprocal knowledge and dialogue rather

[7] Bassam Tibi, "I valori occidentali come unico riferimento" [Western Values as a Unique Reference Point], *Focus*, December 2000.

than what emphasizes differences is fundamental for the promotion of integration and communal solidarity. The authorities must make the effort to establish clear rules to govern coexistence and allow no margin of ambiguity for those who, in the name of "respect for differences", want to build Muslim ghettos within European societies.

C. Minarets in Italy: Requests for Recognition

77.   *The number of resident Muslims in Italy is estimated at around seven hundred thousand people. This population will probably increase because of new arrivals seeking jobs and family reunification and because of the high Muslim birthrate, which is much higher than the Italian average. We are faced with the second-largest religious community in Italy demanding the acknowledgment of its prerogatives from the civil authorities. What would you recommend be done about the situation?*

The phrase "the second-largest religion professed in Italy" might lead a person to think in terms of millions of people. The reality is a community of seven hundred thousand persons, which is 1.2 percent of those who live in Italy.

Defining Italy as a "multireligious" country is ambiguous: the presence of practitioners of faiths apart from Christianity (in its different confessions), such as Islam, Judaism, Buddhism, and Hinduism, does not mean that in the Italian society all faiths have the same weight. Christianity, in Italy, cannot be downgraded to one minor reality among the others, forgetting the contribution that it gave to the creation of Western civilization. This is obvious. The rhetoric of "multi-" (as in "multicultural" or "multireligious") tends to level everything within it to an undifferentiated, unqualified, and anonymous equality. I am aware that what

I am saying is not politically correct, but it is certainly closer to the reality and the history of Italy than certain sociological analyses, which in the name of tolerance and a misunderstood solidarity distort the perspective and lead to wrong conclusions about the juridical and cultural profile.

78.   *Article 8 of the Italian Constitution establishes that the state can enter into agreements with representatives of various religious confessions. For a long time, Islamic organizations have been demanding the opening of negotiations with government officials in order to obtain certain rights. Do you think that these agreements can work?*

The first consideration is a question of method: Who has the right to represent Muslims in Italy? This is a very difficult problem because Islam does not acknowledge any one authority from the juridical point of view. The organizations working in Italy are divided, and each claims the right of representing the needs of the Muslims. Presently, four different Muslim organizations are vying to negotiate an agreement.[8]

The main problem is that, in Italy, Islam is still in an early stage of settlement and community organization that has not developed any popular leadership yet. Therefore, it does not seem wise to me to insist on beginning official negotiations with organizations whose real representative role is uncertain and is sometimes the object of disapproval and criticism. It would perhaps be better to deal unilaterally with the most urgent requests and wait for the emergence of representative leaders of the entire Muslim community before initiating discussions. Any agreement between the Italian state and a religious confession is something very binding

[8] See question 19. Cf. appendix C, "Islam in Italy".

for both parties, and it risks becoming more of an obstacle than a help to solve specific problems. Many problems could be faced in a pragmatic way by simply turning to already-existing laws and local agreements that demand neither the intervention of the state nor that of religious representatives.

79.   *Different Muslim organizations have proposed land grants and public financing for the construction of worship places and mosques; the establishment of autonomous areas for burial inside already-existing cemeteries or for independent Islamic cemeteries; permission to butcher* ḥalāl *meat according to qur'ānic prescriptions; Islamic-compatible menus in schools and workplaces; the teaching of the Muslim religion in the schools; the hiring of Muslim religious staff in hospitals, prisons, and military barracks; excused absences from work or school on the main Muslim holidays and suspension of work for ritual prayer; and civil acknowledgment of marriages celebrated according to the Islamic rite. How should these requests be treated?*

Each request should be dealt with in accord with its compatibility with the Italian juridical system. Key principles, such as the secular state and the distinction between temporal and spiritual order, equality between men and women, and freedom of conscience, must be maintained. These principles are very important preliminary specifications for avoiding an ambiguous approach made in the name of an equally ambiguous multicultural perspective, according to which every social or religious group can claim rights in the name of the defense of minorities and of the respect for different identities.

Some requests made by the Islamic organizations can be accommodated on the basis of the regulations already existing in Italy. The ritual butchering of animals according to

Islamic custom prescribes throat slitting to allow the out-
flow of blood from the flesh. This is already practiced by
butchers in some Italian cities because of hygienic regulations and sanitary laws. Because of the requests made by
numerically large groups of Muslim students, the cafeterias
of some schools offer menu items compatible with their
dietary laws.

The legality of Muslim women having their identity-
document photographs taken while wearing the traditional
Islamic *foulard* is acknowledged by a circular letter of the
Ministry of the Interior, and it is already a standard pro-
cedure. The only government condition on the practice is
that the features of the face are easily and clearly recognizable. Personally, I have some reservations about this practice. Until the 1970s, in the majority of Islamic countries,
women appeared bareheaded in their identity photographs. It is the Islamist radical tendency of the last three
decades that imposed the *foulard* requirement. If the government continues to surrender to such demands, it risks
strengthening the radicals, who claim to be the only authentic Muslims.

The religious assistance provided by Muslim chaplains in
prisons, barracks, or hospitals meets the understandable spiritual needs of the Muslims and can be managed without
difficulties, provided that the criteria of selection and authorization of the religious staff are clearly defined and that its
activity does not exceed the spiritual field.

I am puzzled, however, by the request for separate Islamic
cemeteries. If the final goal is complete social integration,
and if we are trying to learn the difficult task of living
together, why seek separation when life is over? Would not
it be a prophetical sign to pray together side by side in a
cemetery that welcomes all the dead and where everyone is
honored according to his religious tradition?

My responses are not offered from a strictly juridical point of view but are ideas intended to help build up a society of coexistence between different groups instead of a society where every group lives on its own isolated island.

80. *Among the requests advanced by the Islamic organizations is that Friday, the Muslim day of weekly rest, be observed. On Friday, Muslim students would be allowed an absence from school in order to participate in common prayer. There is a similar request that Islamic holidays be observed. How should the authorities proceed in these matters?*

Although it seems paradoxical, in the Islamic tradition the weekly day of rest has no specific religious significance. The belief that God rested on the seventh day of creation, which is the origin of the concept of a weekly day of rest, comes from the Judeo-Christian tradition. It is considered by Muslims an anthropomorphism to be condemned. God never rests, and the Qur'ān does not prescribe rest on Friday. The day of rest in Islamic countries resulted not from religious precepts but from the need to adapt to international work standards, namely to provide for at least one day of rest during the week. The only religious obligation for Friday is for attendance and participation at the public prayer that is held at midday. The service lasts half an hour and normally takes place during lunchtime and is therefore compatible with normal working activities.

As far as the request for the Friday day of rest is concerned, I must mention some recent research conducted by the Fondazione Agnelli in Turin, which verified that in the nations of origin of the majority of Muslims living in Italy, Friday is not the weekly day of rest. Albania, Senegal, Tunisia, and Turkey observe Sunday, while Morocco allows freedom of choice among Friday, Saturday, Sunday, or the market day.[9]

Since the weekly day of rest on Friday has no foundation in Islamic doctrine or is practiced in the countries from which the majority of Muslims living in Italy come, there is no reason for Italy to adjust its calendar to accommodate this request.

81. *What do you think of the request for interrupting work in order to perform ritual prayer?*

The Islamic tradition allows the grouping of the five prayers at any time of the day, especially the first with the second one (which can be done at home, before going to work), and the fourth with the fifth one (which can be done after returning home after work), while during lunchtime it is possible to recite the third one. This is how the majority of Muslims pray each day.

In fact, the Fondazione Agnelli researchers found that no Muslim country, except Saudi Arabia, had legislated on this topic. Almost everywhere, the times for prayer are left to the free initiative of individuals and most often are grouped together so that they can be performed outside of work time. In Italy, some places allow Muslim workers to stop work briefly for their ritual prayer. Such allowances have been granted in the Ragusa province, where non-European immigrants are in some cases 30 percent of the workforce. In other provinces, some employers offer small buildings for Muslim prayer. I think that where there is a meaningful presence of Muslims and a sincere request by

[9] Cf. Roberta Aluffi Beck-Peccoz, *Tempo, lavoro e culto nei Paesi musulmani* [Time, Work and Worship in Islamic Countries] (Turin: Fondazione Giovanni Agnelli, 2000).

Muslim workers, agreements of this kind can work, even in the company's labor negotiations, without appealing to legislative bodies and involving religious authorities. In any case, such permission should be periodically reviewed on the basis of real needs.

Specific agreements between workers and employers regarding work schedule flexibility could be established. This is a topic that needs to be dealt with in a nonconfessional way, in order to help avoid conflicts based on religious principles. It seems better for business owners and workers to look for secular, realistic, and pragmatic solutions that have the purpose of achieving the maximum possible integration.

82.   *What is your response to Muslim requests for the teaching of the Islamic religion in schools?*

It will be necessary to rely on the Italian legal system in order to reach an agreement. The teaching of Islam in the schools requires a series of preliminary steps associated with program content, textbooks, and choice of teachers, which must, in all cases, be under government control and supervision.

Common sense suggests that a minimum number of students be present in a school before organizing a class. Teaching should start only when an explicit request has been made by interested students and their families. It is obvious that the lessons should be given in the Italian language to encourage teacher accountability as well as the process of student integration into the social fabric of the nation. Any requests for teaching classes in Arabic (because it is the language of the Qur'ān and the qur'ānic schools) should be denied.

When Germany permitted the teaching of Islam in its schools, it raised serious problems. In some cases, the appointment of religious teachers was delegated to the government of Turkey because of the preponderance of Turkish students in some schools. This practice implied foreign interference and discrimination against young Muslims of other nationalities in the schools. There also arose the fear that the schools were being infiltrated by teachers connected with the most radical organizations that transform religion lessons into anti-Western exercises.

83. *Another very controversial request is for civil acknowledgment of the* shari'a *marriage, which is celebrated according to the Islamic rite. In your opinion, how should this matter be handled?*

Here we are not facing a question of religious ritual but a substantial civil problem. The Islamic tradition rests on some principles that are in contradiction with the Italian constitution. Islam allows polygamy, with the possibility for Muslim males to contract simultaneously up to four marriages. Problems such as issues of divorce, child custody, inheritance, and the religion of the children also arise. All of these are incompatible with Italian law.[10]

84. *Because of so many incompatibilities of Islamic tradition with the Italian juridical system, should the civil government accept*

[10] See also question 50. A group of experts is preparing a list of proposals to make some aspects of Islamic marriage consistent with Italian law. They seek to introduce a sort of "double track" (according to the religious confession of the citizens) that acknowledges a number of personal prerogatives without any consequences at the civil level. About this, see the contribution by Cristina Campiglio, "Famiglia e diritto islamico: Profili internazionali-privatistici" [Family and Islamic Law: International-Privatistic Profiles], in *L'Islam in Europa: Lo statuto giuridico delle comunità musulmane* [Islam in Europe: The Juridical Status of Muslim Communities], ed. Silvio Ferrari (Bologna: Il Mulino, 2000), 175–85, and another by Pierpaolo Donati, "Le regole per una convivenza possibile: I nodi familiari" [The Rules for a Possible Coexistence: The Family Problems], in *Con-vivere la città* (Bologna: Nautilus, 2000), 67–86.

all the civil effects of Islamic sharīʿa *marriage, or should it recognize the Muslim marriage rite as having religious value only?*

In Islam, the religious and the civil domains are not easily separated. The risk is that of multiplying anomalous situations, which already exist, whereby a Muslim man, already married to a woman from a civil point of view, enters a *sharī-atic* marriage with another woman. Although sharī-atic marriages have no juridical value in Italy, they contribute to the creation of ambiguous situations that can be the sources of abuse and injustice.

According to the rules of international private law, as followed in Italy, the personal and proprietary relations between spouses are regulated by the national law of their native country, and this principle also applies to the relations between parents and children. Therefore, the foreign-born Muslims living in Italian territory are subject to the Islamic law by which they were married in their respective countries of origin.

Here arises an important question, which I think will recur even more frequently with increasing immigration from Islamic countries: Is it appropriate for an Italian judge to apply, always and in every case, the laws that derive from *sharīʿa*, even when they clearly establish the supremacy of man over woman and put clear limitations on the rights of women? Ought not the *sharīʿa* be rejected when it conflicts with the principle of equality between the sexes and therefore is contrary to public order? [11]

It seems wise that even in family matters, we should not encourage the creation of a sort of parallel "community

---

[11] The topic is treated in a systematic and organic way by Roberta Aluffi Beck-Peccoz, ed., *Le leggi del diritto di famiglia negli Stati arabi del Nord-Africa* [The Regulations of Family Law in the North-African Arab States] (Turin: Fondazione Giovanni Agnelli, 1997), 27–31.

law" in accord with the religious confession of various citizen groups.

85. *Taking into account the specific requests that we have examined so far, what is the general rule that should be applied?*

It is absolutely necessary to promote the maximum possible integration of Muslim immigrants into Italian society. Freedom of religious expression must be granted; it is already guaranteed by the Italian Constitution. Italy, however, must avoid imposing special laws and regulations to control Muslims, as often happens to non-Muslims in Islamic countries where the sole reference point is Islam.

Secularism is an achievement that modern society and the nation-state cannot lose. Secularism may represent an opportunity to encourage a process of modernization in the Muslim world that is slowly taking place in the immigrants' nations of origin.

D. The Mosque: A Muslim Church?

86. *The topic of the mosque in Italy periodically inflames discussions and sparks controversies. Italian public opinion commonly holds that the mosque is the Muslim place of worship, and therefore the criteria for the concession of pieces of land or buildings must be similar to those followed for churches. Many people believe that the mosque is simply a "Muslim church". What does the mosque actually represent for a Muslim?*

The statement that "the mosque is a Muslim church" is erroneous. The mosque represents something absolutely and radically different. To understand its meaning and function, one must start, not from the Christian tradition or even from a Western mentality, but from Islam's nature and history.

In the Arabic tradition, there exist two terms to define the mosque: *masjid* (passed into Spanish through the word *mezquita* and from there to the different European languages) and *jāmiᶜ*. This latter word is the more widespread in the Arab-Islamic world. The first word derives from the root *s-j-d*, which means "to prostrate oneself", while the second word derives from the root *j-m-ᶜ*, which means "to gather". The mosque is the place where the community gathers for prayer but also to face whatever is before it, including social, cultural, and political issues. All the decisions of the community are made in the mosque; trying to limit it to a place for prayer represents a complete misunderstanding of Muslim tradition.

Friday (*yawm al-jumuᶜa*) is the day when the community gathers at midday for public prayer, which is followed by the *khuṭba*, that is, the speech. The *khuṭba* cannot be likened to the homily pronounced by the Catholic priest during the Mass, for the *khuṭba* deals with the most relevant issues of the moment, going beyond the spiritual aspects. In many Muslim countries, such as Egypt (the most populated Arab country), the mosques are monitored by the police on Friday. There is a simple reason for this: many political decisions start from the mosque, during the Friday *khuṭba*. Historians of Islam know that many riots and revolutions were launched from the mosques and that *jihād* is often proclaimed during the *khuṭba*. For this reason, many Muslim countries require that the text of the speech must be previously submitted to the civil authorities for approval.

87.   *Do you think it is incorrect to consider the mosque as a place of worship?*

The prevailing view among Muslims must be taken into account. Considering the mosque to be only a place of worship is wrong and restrictive; it is also misleading to talk of the construction of mosques in the name of religious freedom because they are not just religious buildings but are community places that also have a cultural, social, and political function.

One cannot forget that the place consecrated to the prayer on Friday is considered a holy space of Islam and that it is forever the privilege of the community to decide who has permission to be admitted and who would profane it.

In Muslim towns, there are often some small rooms, called *muṣallā*, that are places for prayer (*ṣalāt*). These are "chapels" of a sort that can contain a few dozen faithful and are often located on the ground floor of a house, instead of a flat. These places are more discreet than a mosque and are almost always used solely for the noontime prayer of people who arrive from the street or from nearby houses.

Mosques normally have a minaret tower (*manāra*), where the muezzin (*mu'adhdhin*) calls people to prayer (*adhān*). These minarets have a practical function and are slightly higher than the surrounding houses. Historically, they have the symbolic value of signifying the Muslim presence: the minaret suggests the superiority of Islam over other religions. But the minarets' most essential purpose is allowing the voice of the muezzin to reach those who live in the neighborhood. As of the twentieth century, megaphones or loudspeakers have begun to be installed on the minarets (especially if there is a church or a Christian neighborhood nearby), and the muezzin have added other sentences to the call to prayer, prolonging it. These innovations are contrary to the Muslim tradition, and the most orthodox Islamic countries (e.g., Saudi Arabia) condemn them even though the condemnation does not change well-established habits. In other countries (e.g., Egypt), the use of loudspeakers is exclusively limited to the call to prayer (which lasts about two minutes), but the use of a loudspeaker is forbidden for the call at dawn, a prohibition that is often not observed. The use of recordings for the call to prayer, which is frequent in Europe, is considered contrary to tradition in most Muslim countries.

Apart from all the Muslim historical and "liturgical" considerations about which I have just expounded, it is also good to ask who finances the construction and the maintenance of the mosques. This inquiry is not intended to intrude into somebody else's affairs but is motivated by the principle that states that "those who pay, rule." It is not a secret that the majority of mosques and Islamic centers in Europe are financed by foreign governments, particularly by Saudi Arabia, which also imposes a trustworthy *imām*. It is a well-known fact that in the Sunni Islamic world, Saudi Arabia represents the most rigid tendency, called Wahhabi. I do not think these *A'īma* will help the immigrants either to integrate into Western society or to assimilate modernity, which are necessary preconditions for peaceful coexistence with the native populations.

88.   *What should we do, then? How should we respond to the increasing number of Muslim requests for plots of land on which to build mosques?*

Provided that the legal rules and traditions of the Western societies are respected, "allow Muslims to pray" is the obvious answer. Streets, sidewalks, or squares should not be taken over for prayer, which unfortunately happens in some Muslim countries. This practice is fast becoming widespread in Italy too and is often justified by the fact that there is insufficient room in the mosques for all who are seeking to pray. The non-Muslim residents of a neighborhood ought not to be disturbed at five in the morning or at ten in the evening by the call to prayer through a loudspeaker. Moreover, we must remember that, according to Islamic precepts, one can pray anywhere: at home, in the streets, at work, in the fields. In fact, even for common prayers, it is not necessary to go to the mosque because "the entire world is the big mosque", as Muhammad states in a *ḥadīth*.[12]

In Italy, where Muslim communities are scattered in small towns as well, the best solution seems to be that of *muṣallā*: "chapels" where the faithful can comfortably meet to pray. *Muṣallā* would also be less expensive to construct as compared to large mosque buildings, which need financing from foreign governments or from international Islamic organizations. The only risk with this approach of small prayer centers is that it will be more difficult for the authorities to control the teachings given in them.

Finally, I would like to stress again the fact that the mosque cannot simply be categorized as a place of worship because in the Islamic conception, it is a meeting center with cultural, social, and political aspects. Governments have the duty and the right to monitor carefully the activities that are going on in the rooms that are designated generically as mosques: authorities need to know who are the persons in charge and ask who manages, who controls, and who finances the mosque. Here I am speaking about going beyond the legally required guarantees that must be given to the city, to its inhabitants, and also to those who will attend that place of worship. It is a good antidote to those people who tend to identify any place meant for Muslim prayer as a potential terrorist base or, in

---

[12] See Arent Jan Wensinck and J. P. Mensing, *Concordance et indices de la tradition musulmane* [Concordances and Indexes of the Islamic Tradition], vol. 2 (Leiden: Brill, 1943), saying no. 424a. The saying is quoted in three out of the six great collections: Bukhārī, *Anbiyā'* 40; Muslim, *Masājid* 1, 2, and 3; and Nisā'ī, *Masājid* 3 and 42.

any case, as a place to be treated with suspicion more than with due respect.[13]

E. Models of Integration

89.   *Almost all the industrialized countries of Europe have in recent years been receiving large numbers of immigrants from the Third World. What do you think about the models that have so far been adopted in the West for integrating foreigners into national society?*

Three models have been adopted up to this time.

1. *Assimilation.* According to this scheme, the foreigner must conform not only to the laws and to the language of the host country but also to its culture and behavior. The immigrant must renounce all of his peculiarities. Basically, it is the French prescription, proposed in the name of the secular society that makes everybody theoretically equal before the state. This proposition has many limits because it implies and requires a complete identification of citizens with the state. This is in fact impossible to realize or to manage in reality.

2. *The melting pot.* This is the American model, in which immigrants blend with the local population, maintaining some prerogatives of their culture. This model has the quality of strengthening the newly arrived minorities' sense of belonging to the greatest nation in the world, giving them a legitimate pride in the flag and the national anthem and

[13] For a deeper analysis, see Samir Khalil Samir, "La moschea: Informazione e riflessione" [The Mosque: Information and Reflections], *Avvenire*, December 8, 2000; and "Note sulla moschea" [Notes on the Mosque], *La Civiltà Cattolica* 152, I, 3618 (2001): 599–603.

participation in the collective achievements of the country.

However, the melting pot is manifesting its limits right now because of the new migratory waves and the different rates of demographic growth among the various ethnic communities. This is creating a problem with the commonly shared values of the white Anglo-Saxon Protestant (WASP) culture that formed the core of American society. Those that were once minority groups are fast ascending to be majorities and are claiming their rights and power. This phenomenon is upsetting the traditional well-established social balance.

3. *The multicultural society.* Great attention is paid in Europe to the third model, multiculturalism, which is based on the principles that all cultures have equal dignity and can easily coexist and that the plurality of expressions is a sign of the richness and a guarantee of improvement of society.

This position can be summarized with a slogan: "Different is beautiful." It originates from cultural relativism, which generates juridical relativism, which is the attempt to give legitimacy to the diversities that characterize the minorities recently arrived in Europe. Everything seems to work well as long as we remain on the theoretical plane. However, if we think of the logical and practical consequences of the multicultural position, many incongruities arise.

If I say to an Egyptian immigrant, Your culture is very beautiful, you have a background of centuries of civilization, preserve your Egyptian identity and do not worry about integrating because the Italians will be enriched by your diversity, it is logical that the Egyptian immigrant will do his best to congregate with his fellow countrymen, talk to them in his native language, and in general attempt to live as if he were still in Egypt. All immigrant groups across the globe attempt to recreate a microcosm of their native country in their neighborhoods or ghettos. For the young, the problem is the tension that develops between the native culture—maintained in the family home and neighborhood—and the host country culture, with which young people tend to identify. At school, they learn to become Italians, but at home they speak, eat, and live as if they were back in Cairo. This creates a destabilizing situation for social coexistence. It risks increasing conflicts and making the negotiation of differences even more difficult. I am convinced that the multicultural model resembles more a dangerous utopia than an ideal to be pursued.

90. *What do you mean by the phrase "a multicultural utopia"? From what does the idea derive?*

At its origin, there is a series of concomitant factors often connected by cause-and-effect relationships. There is the very human desire that aspires to the new, to the novel and fresh, which is indicative of a thirst for knowledge of reality in all of its multiplicity. Unfortunately, this can easily degenerate into cheap exoticism, into the admiration of everything that is different and new. This tendency is growing increasingly pronounced in the West.

There also exists a relativistic attitude that derives from the crisis of the ideological and religious uncertainties characterizing the contemporary age and leading to a tendency to blame whatever is "traditional".

Finally, there is a guilt complex (which I prefer to call "mea-culpism") that is very widespread in the West regarding the colonial experiences of the Third World nations. This complex goes so far as to justify the acceptance of any cultural "import" in the name of relativism or simply because "in their country this is the way they behave." Promoters of this position claim that extra-European cultures, which were subjugated in the past, must not be discriminated against today. Neither should Europeans oppose those people who want to transplant their cultures to the West today.

These are some of the premises of multiculturalism, and the results are evident for the entire world to see. In particular, these premises penalize the Christian host culture. In the name of respect for religious differences and of the defense of minorities, Christians are required to take the crucifix off hospital walls, to give up building the manger in classrooms at Christmastime, and to choose nonreligious poems or songs for the school Christmas pageant performance. In addition to this discrimination against a great majority of the students, in the name of multiculturalism Muslims and those students of other faiths are also prevented from knowing fundamental elements of Western history and civilization that are more cultural in nature than confessional. These forms of self-censorship are harmful and nourish conflicts instead of controlling them and indicate very real identity problems in those who promote them.

91.   *What is the most adequate model for realizing an authentic integration of immigrants into Italy?*

Only when an initial "solid core" (a reference background at the anthropological level) is attained can foreign communities amalgamate, that is to say, integrate with the founding elements. With a strong core, we can prevent civil coexistence from wildly evolving according to an undifferentiated egalitarianism or according to the soulless relativism advanced by the supporters of the multicultural society.

If I had to give a name to this model of coexistence, I would call it the "model of the enriched identity". It derives from the awareness that in each individual there is a cultural and anthropological element that grew over centuries and that produces a certain way of considering the human being and of organizing coexistence, work, play, and worship. It is a background identity that we cannot forget or abandon if we want to plan and attain a new form of society. This identity is not something fixed and immutable in time but is a developing reality that, while preserving its constitutive characteristics, is capable of integrating elements from other cultures that are compatible with it and of receiving and amalgamating the new elements that it encounters along the way and being enriched by them. It takes a long time to realize an authentic integration. Clear acceptance of the rules by those who arrive from abroad is certainly necessary. If the host society does not have a clear idea of its own identity, it will not be able to integrate others into itself easily. In fact, it will become overly anxious with the new and see in it a threat to its safety.

Xenophobia originates from the fear that what is "different" puts at risk an already-fragile coexistence simply because the "other" is not founded on sound values and certainties. Xenophobia operates on emotion in a vacuum of values and is a real indicator of the fragility, weakness, and insecurity of the host culture. For this reason, the migratory waves and the growth of the Islamic communities represent a true and difficult challenge not only for Italian society but for all of Europe, which is obliged to wonder about its cultural-historical makeup and the ideals and values that define it as a group, as a nation, and as a unique part of the human community.

V. Islam and Christianity: The Unavoidable Encounter, the Possible Dialogue

A. Islam and Other Religions

92. *How does Islam relate to other world religions, especially the monotheistic ones?*

Humanity, in the classic Muslim understanding, is divided into three categories.

The first category is the believers (*mu'minūn*), that is, Muslims. The second category is the protected peoples (*dhimmī*). These are Christians, Jews, and Sabaeans,[1] who are considered monotheists but imperfect believers. They can preserve their faith without being obliged to convert to Islam. However, they must be subjugated, as it is recommended by some verses of the Qur'ān that warn believers to guard against becoming friends with them or giving them power over Muslims. The third category is that of polytheists, the unbelievers (*kāfirūn or kuffār*). These people must be fought,

---

[1] Some scholars add to the *dhimmī* the Zoroastrians, who are mentioned only once in the Qur'ān (Pilgrimage, sura 22:17) under the name of *majūs* (magi). The Sabaeans are a confession that does not exist anymore, probably corresponding to a Baptist Jewish-Christian sect of the first centuries, the Mandaeans. They are not to be mistaken with the Sabians of Harrān, who were astral worshippers, or with the inhabitants of the ancient kingdom of Sheba, in Yemen. See Carlo Alfonso Nallino, the "Sabii" entry of the *Enciclopedia Italiana* (Rome, 1936), 30:379ff. See also Baron B. Carra de Vaux, the "Sābi'a" entry of the *Encyclopédie de l'Islam* (Leiden: Brill, 4:21ff).

and the only alternative to death for them is the conversion to Islam.

Therefore, the Muslim jurists divide the world into three parts that correspond to these categories: *dār al-silm* (the House of Peace), *dār al-ṣulḥ* (the House of Protection), and *dār al-ḥarb* (the House of War). Historically, Muslims were obliged to make some adjustments in their principles to make them compatible with the rapid expansion of Islamic domination. After conquering India, they could not convert all the inhabitants, nor could they kill all those who did not convert.[2] Therefore, they were obliged to perform juridical acrobatics in order to let other religions enter the category of protected peoples. Some jurists noticed that some of the other religions were not mentioned in the Qur'ān and so decided to evaluate each case separately.

The Qur'ān contains both favorable and less-than-favorable verses regarding Christians and Jews. However, Christians are always considered in a more positive manner when compared with Jews, for a historical reason: Arab and Ethiopian Christians who lived in Mecca at the time of Muhammad were in charge of defending the city. When Muhammad first encountered opposition, he sent his followers to Ethiopia, the seat of a Christian kingdom at that time, where they were welcomed with generosity. For this reason, Islam maintained, for some time, a very positive attitude toward Christians. This is witnessed by the qur'ānic verse "You will find that the most implacable of men in their enmity to the faithful [that is, to the Muslims] are the Jews and the pagans, and that the nearest in affection to them are those who say: 'We are Christians.' That is because

---

[2] Islam reached the delta of the Indus River in 713 and officially entered the history of the Indian subcontinent with Mahmūd of Ghazna's (998–1030) conquest.

there are priests[3] and monks among them; and because they are free from pride."[4]

Muhammad had contact with the Jews, especially after his 622 migration to Medina, where rich and powerful Jewish tribes lived. At the beginning, the relations were good: he even chose Jerusalem, like the Jews, as the *qibla* (the orientation point for his followers' prayer) and Yôm Kippūr as a fasting day. But around the end of the year 2 of Hegira (623 of the Christian era), he changed strategy and broke relations with the Jews. The *qibla* was established in the direction of Mecca, and the fasting was extended to the month of Ramaḍān. It was a tactical move to conquer the Arabs: in fact, he intended to underline the fact that he was not against the role of Mecca as a religious center but was rather against the polytheism of its inhabitants.

Muhammad succeeded in his intention "to retrieve" polytheism from the religious point of view. He preserved almost all the pagan rites of the traditional pilgrimage to Mecca: the running from one hill to another one, the walking around the Kaʿba seven times, the launching of stones in the valley, the drinking of the water of the Zamzam fountain, and so on. He preserved these rites but gave them a new meaning, connecting them to rituals practiced by Abraham and Ishmael.[5] It was a fantastic enculturation of Islam in pagan Arab society. The rites of the pilgrimage to Mecca are all of pagan origin but are Islamized, to the point that the famous theologian al-Ghazālī, in "The Proof of Islam", wrote: "The pilgrimage is the most irrational thing in Islam.

---

[3] "Devoted to study" is the Muslim translation for the Arab *qissīsūn*, a Syriac word corresponding to the Greek *presbyteri* (elders). For the Christians, the word always meant "priests".

[4] The Table, sura 5:82.

[5] For Muslims, it is Ishmael and not Isaac whom Abraham was preparing to sacrifice.

There we perform gestures and rites that are absolutely irrational. For this reason, the pilgrimage is the place where we can, better than in any other place, demonstrate our faith because reason does not understand anything at all of it and only faith makes us do those actions. Blind obedience to God is the best evidence of our Islam."[6] A really interesting passage.

93.   How does the break between Muhammad and the faithful of the other two monotheistic religions take place?

There is no break, from the theological point of view, because there was never a unity. Neither the Jews nor the Christians accredited Muhammad as a prophet. They believe that "there is no other god but God", equal to the first part of the Islamic profession of faith. However, neither Jews nor Christians acknowledged Muhammad as a prophet. Unlike Christians, the Jews were a political and economic power in Medina. In al-Medina, the Jews were organized into three main tribes,[7] together with other smaller groups, all rich. In order to increase his power, Muhammad needed to change the situation so that if the Jews refused to recognize his prophecy, they would be chased away. This demonstrates the extent to which the problem was political.

At the beginning, Muhammad kept these Jewish tribes at a distance, but later he attacked the most powerful of them, obliging the survivors to escape to Syria. After a few years, he expelled in succession the other two tribes from the city, preventing them from taking their possessions.

---

[6] See Abū Ḥāmid al-Ghazālī, *Iḥyā' ʿulūm al-dīn* [The Revival of the Religious Sciences], vol. 1, bk. 7, chap. 3, sec. 2 (Cairo, 1939), 272ff.; (Beirut: Dār al-kutub al-ʿilmiyya, 1992), 315.

[7] Banū Qurayẓa, Banū al-Naḍīr (in the Khaybar oasis), and i Banū Qaynuqāʿ.

Muhammad's reason for slaughtering the first tribe was their failure to respect the solidarity agreement with him, but this sounds more like an excuse. The final defeat of the Jews took place during the expedition against the rich Khaybar oasis, in the year 7 of Hegira (A.D. 628). In that period, Muhammad was at his full military ascent and was preparing to enter Mecca.

All this left an echo in the Qur'ān. Verse 82 of the Table, sura 5, compares Jews and Christians: the former are considered enemies, and the latter, friends. But there are other verses that consider both groups as enemies of Muslims. The same sura at verse 51 directs: "Believers, take neither the Jews nor the Christians for your friends. They are friends with one another. Whoever of you seeks their friendship shall become one of their number. God does not guide the wrongdoers." Verse 110 of the 'Imrāns, sura 3, addresses Muslims, saying: "You are the noblest community ever raised up for mankind. You enjoin justice and forbid evil. You believe in God. Had the People of the Book accepted the Faith, it would surely have been better for them. Some are true believers, but most of them are evil-doers." The famous verse 29 of Repentance, sura 9, invites Muslims to fight "against such of those to whom the Scriptures were given" and establishes the payment of the tribute on the part of Christians and Jews, specifying that it must be done "out of hand" and that the people must be "utterly subdued", which means that a master could not, for example, send his servant with the money and that a gesture demonstrating submission was required.

From the start, the relation between Islam and the other two monotheistic religions is ambiguous. In fact, while the enmity between Muslims and Jews was evident, the relation with Christians fluctuated between friendship and hostility, depending on the sociopolitical situation. The Qur'ān often adopts contradictory positions according to the circumstances: sometimes Christians are considered friends; sometimes they must be fought. But since the conquered population was, in the majority of cases, Christian, Islam was obliged to be more tolerant with Christianity on the political plain. On the theological plain, however, Islam and Judaism are relatively similar in the "absolute" conception of monotheism, while Islam and Christianity diverge above all with regard to the trinitarian conception of God and Christ's divinity.

94.   *The Qur'ān uses the word "Nazarenes" to speak of Christians. Many scholars identify the Nazarenes as a Jewish-Christian sect of the time. Is the negative theological judgment on Christianity perhaps connected to this? From which sources did Muhammad derive his biblical knowledge?*

Indeed, the Qur'ān does not know a category of Christians different from that of the "Nazarenes". In Arabic, *al-Naṣārā* is a word that very likely derives from *al-Nāṣira* (Nazareth). Certainly the beliefs of Christians, as they are mentioned by the Qur'ān, do not correspond with any of the great Christian communities of the time, that is, the Nestorians, Monophysites, or Chalcedonians.[8] There are two possible interpretations: the first one consists in the fact that the Arab-Christians lived on the fringes of the Christian world, being

---

[8] Nestorius made a distinction between Christ's humanity and divinity, and he refused to call Mary *Theotokos*, Mother of God, preferring the title "Mother of Christ". The Monophysites followed Patriarch Dioscorus of Alexandria in the theory that Christ has only one nature (*physis*). According to them, Christ came from two natures, but after his Incarnation, there was only "one nature incarnated in the Word of God". In 451 the Monophysite doctrine was condemned at the Council of Chalcedon, which proclaimed that Christ is true God and true man.

dispersed in the vast Arabic peninsula, without ecclesiastical organization; the second one lies in a certain difficulty on Muhammad's part in understanding the nature and the content of the main Christian dogmas.

Islamic understanding of Christianity does not follow the theology of any of the three Christian denominations mentioned above. It seems closer to the Arian position, which denies the full divinity of Christ. This may be the reason the great theologian Saint John Damascene, who in the eighth century lived among Muslims first in Damascus and then in Jerusalem, mistook Islam for a new Christian sect. This mistake was not committed by any Eastern theologian, either Syriac or Arab, but only by some Greek and Latin theologians.

The biblical accounts contained in the Qur'ān are almost all drawn from the canonical and apocryphal books of the Old Testament and the Gospels. The account of the Annunciation in the Qur'ān, for example, resembles the one quoted in the Gospel, while the miracles performed by Jesus as a young boy or even the account of Mary's nativity are drawn from the apocryphal "infancy gospels", which seem to have been widespread among the Christian pre-Islamic Arabs.

The Islamic interpretation of the dogmatic aspects of Christianity cannot be found in any of the Christian traditions, not even in the heretical ones. For example, when the Qur'ān says that the Christian Trinity is formed by God, Jesus, and Mary,[9] it is impossible to find a sect ever stating this. The only hypothesis that I can formulate is that we are faced with a distorted interpretation of the Christian

---

[9] See the Table, sura 5:116: "Then God will say: Jesus son of Mary, did you ever say to mankind: Worship me and my mother as gods besides God?"

theological statements about Mary as the Mother of God and about Jesus the Son of God. It was quite logical for Muslims to conceive these dogmas according to a story line from Arab mythology: a god takes a wife, and they conceive another god.

A confirmation of this hypothesis is the criticism addressed in the Qur'ān to Christians for maintaining that God had a concubine (*Ṣāḥiba*, that is, a mate): "He (exalted be the glory of our Lord!) has taken no consort, nor has He begotten any children";[10] "Creator of the heavens and the earth. How should He have a son when He had no consort? He created all things, and He has knowledge of all things." [11] Or the famous verses of sura 19, Mary, that condemn the idea of God begetting a son. "God forbid that He Himself should beget a son! When He decrees a thing He need only say: 'Be,' and it is";[12] "Those who say: 'The Lord of Mercy has begotten a son,' preach a monstrous falsehood.... That they should ascribe a son to the Merciful, when it does not become the Lord of Mercy to beget one!" [13]

Moreover, the small chapter of the pure faith, or of the sincere worship (Oneness, sura 112), states, "Say: 'God is One, the Eternal God. He begot none, nor was He begotten. None is equal to Him'." This sura is the traditional answer to the Christian Creed, which says, "begotten, not made", even if we know that those verses were pronounced in Mecca against the pagans and not against Christians.

The Qur'ān condemns any idea of divine paternity because it perceives paternity as a physical generation, the outcome of sexual intercourse.

[10] The Jinn, sura 72:3.
[11] Cattle, sura 6:101.
[12] Mary, sura 19:35.
[13] Ibid., 19:88–92.

95.   *Because Christians are believed to ascribe partners to God in the Trinity, Muslims do not consider Christians monotheists. Is that correct?*

Christians are considered believers, even if imperfect ones. The verses that are an invitation to fight them are the product of historical–political circumstances. Unfortunately, this is the ambiguity of the Qur'ān and of Islam, which mixes principles with concrete situations. One can quote many *ḥadīth* ascribed to Muhammad that are very benign toward Jews and Christians, while others are less so. One of them tells that Muhammad stood up as a sign of respect when a funeral procession passed in front of him, and when someone pointed out that the dead was Jewish, he replied: "So what? Does he not have a soul?" A recommendation contained in another *ḥadīth* says, "Whoever wrongs a *dhimmī*, I will be his accuser in the Day of Judgment." Still another says, "Whoever kills a *dhimmī* will never smell the perfume of Paradise." [14] Christians are, in fact, "under the protection of God and of his messenger", and Muhammad recommended that his generals respect all the agreements made with them and not impose burdens that exceed their capacity for endurance.

However, there are other *ḥadīth* hostile to Christians, such as that in which Muhammad claimed he received the order to fight people until they profess that there is no other divinity but God[15] and (in another version of the same saying) that "Muhammad is God's Messenger." [16] Apart from the controversial saying that announces the expulsion of Jews and Christians from the Arabic peninsula, we find a *ḥadīth*

[14] This is a perfume that, according to the same *ḥadīth*, lasts for forty years of wandering.
[15] See Bukhārī, chapter on *zakāt*, 24,1; and chapter on *jihād*, 56,102: *Umirtu an uqātila an-nāsa hattā yaqūlū "Lā ilāha illā Allāh"*.
[16] See Bukhārī, chapter on faith, 2,17.

that declares "there is no Church in Islam" or even that "there is no monastic life in Islam." Another one states that no church should be erected in Muslim lands and that no damaged or ruined one should be restored.

Another saying recommends that Muslims should never be the first to greet Christians and Jews. The saying actually specifies that if you meet them on your path, you should oblige them to walk the hardest way. This is a *hadīth* that periodically comes to the fore. In the late 1990s, the Muslim Brotherhood disseminated a hostile message in both schools and offices throughout Egypt and Jordan, ordering the Muslims not to greet Christians or offer them good wishes for Easter and Christmas. The mother of a Lebanese child personally verified with the school director the truthfulness of her son's account, and she was shocked. When the Lebanese ambassador reported the fact to King Ḥussein of Jordan, he immediately dismissed the teacher. Many behaviors imbued with fanaticism are inspired by such sayings as this one. The attitude of Islam toward Christianity is therefore ambiguous, and this contributes to making coexistence between the faithful of the two religions difficult.

B. Jesus and Muhammad: Two Prophets?

96.   *Islam considers Jesus among the most important prophets in the history of humanity. How is his life presented in the Qur'ān?*

Muhammad elaborated an image of Jesus coherent with the way the Qur'ān presents the biblical prophets but different from the one presented by the evangelists in the Gospels in many important aspects.

The Qur'ān recognizes that Jesus is conceived by a virgin "exalted ... above womankind"[17] without the intervention of a man. God, through an angel who appeared in the form of a perfect man, announces to Mary "a Word from Him. His name is the Messiah, Jesus son of Mary";[18] that is, God announces the birth of a "noble child" who will be instructed "in the Scriptures and in wisdom, in the Torah and in the Gospel".[19]

The Qur'ān asserts that Mary gives birth to her child near a palm tree. Then, carrying him in her arms, she takes him to her people, who accuse her of a "strange thing" since she is not married.[20] At this point, miraculously, the child starts speaking to defend his mother and says: "I am the servant of God. He has given me the Book and ordained me a prophet." This and other miracles of Baby Jesus are derived from the apocryphal gospels, from which Muhammad drew inspiration for his presentation of Christ.

Jesus works many miracles, more than any other prophet: he heals the man born blind and the leper, and he raises the dead; but after each miracle, the Qur'ān underlines that he does it "with God's permission".

Jesus is introduced as a man sent to the sons of Israel to remind them of God's message. Around him, we find some disciples that the Qur'ān sometimes refers to as *Anṣār*, or auxiliaries, the same term used by Muhammad to define his followers in Medina. Moreover, as it happens for other prophets, including Moses and Muhammad himself, the majority of Jesus' people do not

---

[17] The 'Imrāns, sura 3:42.
[18] Ibid., 3:45.
[19] Ibid., 3:48.
[20] Mary, sura 19:27.

acknowledge him and reject his teachings, accusing him of sorcery.[21]

Finally, the Qur'ān denies Christ's crucifixion by the Jews and alludes to the supernatural substitution of his person with another, nonspecified one. In sura 4, verse 157, of Women, one reads the ambiguous statement, "They did not kill him, nor did they crucify him, but they thought they did." Hence, according to the Qur'ān, Jesus was not killed but was lifted up to God,[22] and he will come back on the day of Resurrection.

97.   *One can therefore speak of a real qur'ānic Christology. What are its main aspects?*

The qur'ānic theology of Christ is based on a fundamental statement: he is the greatest and the holiest prophet sent by God before Muhammad, but he is just a prophet. Many are the attributes that define him—the Christ,[23] one of the nearest to God, eminent, Word of truth, servant of God, a Sign of the Hour,[24] God's spirit, spirit of sanctity—yet none of these titles acknowledges Christ's divine origin.

When Christians say that Jesus is the Word of God, they mean that he is the eternal Word, coexisting with God, "eternally begotten of the Father", since the Word of God is inseparable from the Father's substance. For Muslims, on the other hand, "Word of God" means that Jesus is the

[21] "This is but plain sorcery!" See the Table, sura 5:110; Cattle, sura 6:7; Jonah, sura 10:76; and Hūd, sura 11:7.

[22] See Women, sura 4:158: "God lifted him up to Him."

[23] "The Christ" is always found with the definite article. This title in the Qur'ān applies only to Jesus. It can be found eleven times in the text, sometimes under the formula "the Christ, son of Mary".

[24] This title can be found only once in the Qur'ān (Ornaments of Gold, sura 43:61), and it applies only to Jesus. It is interpreted in the sense that Jesus is the Sign that announces the end of times.

concrete fruit of God's Word; that is, God said, "Be", and Jesus was. Consequently, Jesus is a man who was born by God's command. To say that Jesus is "God's spirit", *rūḥ min Allāh*, simply means for Muslim commentators, from Tabari to Zamakhshari to Rāzī,[25] that he is pure because he was born without human intervention through the annunciation of God's angel (*rūḥ*).

The same reduction of meaning can be noticed in the word "sign".[26] In fact, the qur'ānic Jesus not only carries a sign to men, but he himself is a sign for men, as affirmed in verse 91 of the Prophets, sura 21: "And of the woman who kept her chastity. We breathed into her of Our spirit, and made her and her son a sign to all mankind." The virginal conception of Christ, however, is not a proof of Jesus' divinity but only a sign of God's might, which makes of his prophet, in this aspect, a noble creature similar to Adam.[27]

Also, miracles are considered the demonstration of God's might and of the divine goodness toward man but not an evidence of the divinity of their performer. Jesus does not work any miracles of himself, but it is God who allows him to perform them or who uses him to perform them. This reasoning can be applied to all the other qur'ānic verses presenting Jesus as someone who declares lawful what was unlawful, or affirming that he was "lifted up to him", although in the Qur'ān this last expression refers uniquely to Jesus.

In the Qur'ān, we find some of the healings and resurrections quoted in the canonical Gospels but also other miracles quoted only in the apocryphal gospels, such as the

---

[25] Commentators of the tenth, twelfth, and thirteenth centuries, respectively.

[26] *Āya* in Arabic. We find it three times in the Qur'ān: 19:21; 21:91; 23:50.

[27] See the 'Imrāns, sura 3:59: "Jesus is like Adam in the sight of God. He created him from dust and then said to him: 'Be', and he was."

episode in which Baby Jesus makes a clay bird fly. In fact, Jesus says in the Qur'ān: "From clay I will make for you the likeness of a bird. I shall breathe into it and, by God's leave, it shall become a living bird." [28] The interesting thing is the double action of creating and breathing, which in the Qur'ān is typically divine.[29] The verb "to create" is quoted 177 times, always as a specific act of God, apart from the 2 times it is used in reference to Jesus. In this, we can perhaps detect a trace of the doctrine of Christ's divinity, despite the contrary affirmation of Islam. It is probably with the intention of eluding this idea that some translate the Arabic verb *khalaqa* (to create) with "mold".

Christ is presented as an authentic Muslim: he teaches absolute monotheism and, consequently, total submission to God, the only Lord. In other words, he teaches Islam and its precepts: almsgiving, prayer, and piety toward parents. Furthermore, Jesus strongly rejects the idea of being God. Verse 116 of the Table, sura 5, is emblematic: "Then God will say: Jesus son of Mary, did you ever say to mankind: 'Worship me and my mother as gods besides God?'" And Jesus answered: "Glory be to You.... I could never have claimed what I have no right to." Christ asks his disciples to obey him but only as a leader, not as the Lord, because "God is my Lord and your Lord: therefore serve Him. That is a straight path." [30]

In the Qur'ān, the prophet Jesus announces the coming of Muhammad. In fact, he says to the sons of Israel, "I am sent forth to you from God to confirm the Torah already

[28] The 'Imrāns, sura 3:49.

[29] "Your Lord said to the angels: I am creating man from dry clay, from black molded loam. When I have fashioned him and breathed of My spirit into him, kneel down and prostrate yourselves before him" (Al-Hijr, sura 15:29).

[30] Mary, sura 19:36.

revealed, and to give news of an apostle that will come
after me whose name is Ahmad." [31] In Arabic, the word
"Ahmad" is another form of "Muhammad"; both mean "the
praised". In the announcement made by Jesus to the apostles regarding the future coming of the "Consoler" (the Holy
Spirit), Muslims read a prophecy about Muhammad. The
origin of this interpretation can be traced back to the Syriac translation of the term "consoler" (*menaḥḥemana*), which
can be found in the Syrian-Palestinian version of the Gospel of Saint John, and not to the corruption of the Greek
parakletos (which means "consoler") to *periklytos* (which means
"praised", that is, Muhammad), as is commonly believed.
In Muslim theology, probably influenced by Christian theology, there is the idea that the authentic prophet is always
announced by those who came before, and this is why Muslim theologians try to find in the Old and in the New Testaments some indications of Muhammad's coming. In reality,
however, this is an artificial operation, for they make arbi-
trary applications of some verses as referring to Muhammad.[32]

---

[31] Battle Array, sura 61:6.

[32] With regard to the different conception of Jesus, the Christ, there is a
significant affirmation made by John Paul II in the book-interview with Vit-
torio Messori, *Crossing the Threshold of Hope* (New York: Alfred A. Knopf,
1994; in Italian as *Varcare la soglia della speranza* [Milan: Mondadori, 1994]).
After remembering that, "thanks to their monotheism", Muslims are "particularly close" to Christians, John Paul II underlines that

> whoever knows the Old and New Testament, and then reads the
> Qur'ān, clearly sees *the process by which it completely reduces Divine Rev-*
> *elation*. It is impossible not to note the movement away from what
> God said about Himself, first in the Old Testament through the proph-
> ets, and then finally in the New Testament through His Son. In Islam
> all the richness of God's self-revelation, which constitutes the heritage
> of the Old and New Testament, has definitely been put aside.
>
> Some of the most beautiful names in the human language are given
> to the God of the Qur'ān, but He is ultimately a God outside of the
> world, a God who is *only Majesty, never Emmanuel*, God-with-us. *Islam*

98. *How are the Gospels presented in the Qur'ān?*

The Qur'ān uses a single word, *Injīl*, always singular, which is the contraction of "Evangel", and it is not used in the plural form *Anājīl*, the Gospels. The Qur'ān does not cite the other books of the New Testament—not even minimal allusion is made to the Acts of the Apostles, the Letters of Paul, or the Apocalypse. When the Qur'ān talks of *Injīl*, it does not refer to a specific book but to Jesus' teaching. I personally believe that in Muhammad's time, there was no complete Arab version of the Gospels available.[33] Muhammad knew only that Christians and Jews had a holy book, and he probably saw a Syriac-language copy of the Gospels.

The qur'ānic attitude toward the Gospels is ambiguous. In fact, Muhammad often invites the pagan Arabs to refer to the "people of the Scriptures" in order to find a confirmation of what he preaches, and he exhorts the Muslim Arabs to address Jews and Christians when they have doubts on the interpretation of the qur'ānic texts.[34] However, Jews and Christians in particular are accused of falsifying their religious texts. The reason is simple: while the Qur'ān "pretends" that Christ announced Muhammad, there is no

is not a religion of redemption. There is no room for the Cross and the Resurrection. Jesus is mentioned, but only as a prophet who prepares for the last prophet, Muhammad. There is also a mention of Mary, His Virgin Mother, but the tragedy of redemption is completely absent. For this reason not only the theology but also the anthropology of Islam is very distant from Christianity. (English ed., 92ff.; Italian ed., 103ff.)

[33] The discussions among scholars on the existence of a complete text of the Gospels in Arabic before Islam are still open. By late 2007, there have been about ten studies published on this topic. However, the majority of the scholars are opposed to this hypothesis.

[34] Cf. the Prophets, sura 21:7: "Ask the People of the Book if you do not know this."

announcement in the Gospels of the coming of a prophet after Christ. In addition, there are many contradictions between the Gospels and the Qur'ān. Hence, it is difficult for Muslims to accept the Christian Bible as authentic. However, the verses of the Gospels that are in agreement with the Qur'ān are accepted by the Muslim tradition. Those verses that disagree with qur'ānic teachings are interpreted allegorically or in a reductive way by excluding a transcendental dimension, or they are simply rejected as the fruit of falsifications. As far as the other books of the New Testament are concerned, they are not only unknown in the Qur'ān but are often ignored or opposed by Muslim scholars and authors. Paul, in particular, is treated as a "black sheep" among Muslims, as one who falsified Christ's message.

99.   *What are the fundamental aspects of Christianity that are denied by Islam?*

The Qur'ān denies the doctrinal foundations of the Christian religion: Christ's divinity, the Incarnation, the crucifixion, the redemption, and the Trinity. If it had ignored them, we could say that silence does not mean a denial, but it explicitly denies them.

By denying Christ's divinity, the Qur'ān meant to save God's honor and Jesus' reputation. Therefore, in different places, the Qur'ān asserts that it is inconceivable that God has children. Some examples are: "Creator of the heavens and the earth. How should He have a son when He had no consort? He created all things, and He has knowledge of all things." [35] "Say: 'Praise be to God who has never begotten a son; who has no partner in His Kingdom; who needs none to defend Him from humiliation.' Proclaim

[35] Cattle, sura 6:101.

His greatness." [36] "Never has God begotten a son, nor is there any other god besides Him." [37] "Sovereign of the heavens and the earth, who has begotten no children and has no partner in His sovereignty." [38]

For a similar reason, the Qur'ān denies the crucifixion. The scandal of the Cross is unacceptable; so God exalted his prophet by raising him to heaven before the crucifixion.

However, it is the concept of the Trinity that constitutes the greatest scandal. In the Qur'ān, there are many polemical verses aimed at Christians about this issue. "Unbelievers are those that say: 'God is one of three'. There is but one God. If they do not desist from so saying, those of them that disbelieve shall be sternly punished." [39] Or again: "People of the Book, do not transgress the bounds of your religion. Speak nothing but the truth about God. The Messiah, Jesus son of Mary, was no more than God's apostle and His Word which He cast to Mary: a spirit from Him. So believe in God and His apostles and do not say: 'Three'. Forbear, and it shall be better for you. God is but one God. God forbid that He should have a son!" [40]

The same appeal addressed by the Qur'ān to Christians rests on the implicit exclusion of the trinitarian notion of God: "People of the Book, let us come to an agreement: that we will worship none but God, that we will associate none with Him, and that none of us shall set up mortals as deities besides God." [41] It would be unacceptable to take the Muslim pretension of teaching Christians their own

[36] The Night Journey, sura 17:111.
[37] The Believers, sura 23:91.
[38] Al-Furqān, sura 25:2.
[39] The Table, sura 5:73.
[40] Women, sura 4:171.
[41] The 'Imrāns, sura 3:64.

faith[42] or the qur'ānic image of Jesus as a point of departure for a sincere Muslim-Christian dialogue. In fact, instead of being a point of encounter between the two religions, the qur'ānic Christology becomes a stumbling block, because Islam thinks it knows who Christ is, starting from the Qur'ān.

The Muslim often thinks of himself as being subject to an injustice and asks the Christian, "Why do I recognize Christ as a prophet while you do not recognize Muhammad as a prophet?" It is difficult to explain that recognizing Jesus as a prophet is reductive for Christians, since for Christians Jesus is the Son of God made man. And this cannot be stated by a Muslim because he would no longer be coherent or true to his faith.

In fact, saying that Jesus is a prophet is not a major revelation for a Muslim since God sent prophets to all the peoples of the earth. The Qur'ān names only twenty-eight prophets, but the Muslim tradition claims that there are hundreds, the last one being Muhammad, the "Seal of the Prophets", as the Qur'ān solemnly declares.[43] This is unacceptable for Christians because it means that Muhammad came to complete and correct what was revealed by Jesus: a statement contrary to the teachings of Jesus himself, who in the Gospels presents himself as the fulfillment of revelation. Indeed, Jesus announces that after him there will be many false prophets. For Christians the "Seal of the Prophets" is John the Baptist, because he not only announced the coming of Christ, as other prophets did before him, but also indicated to his contemporaries, "He is the Messiah." [44]

---

[42] Cf. the Table, sura 5:75: "See how we make plain to them Our revelations. See how they ignore the truth."

[43] The Confederate Tribes, sura 33:40.

[44] Cf. Samir Khalil Samir, "Cristo nel Corano" [Christ in the Qur'ān], *La Civiltà Cattolica* 134, III, n. 3191 (1983): 450–62; and, by the same author,

100.   *How can the figure of Muhammad be considered from a Christian point of view?*

From the reading both of the Qur'ān and of the *ḥadīth*, Muhammad appears as a man who, at the age of forty, had an extraordinary experience in his relationship with God that deeply changed his life and compelled him to devote himself to making his experience known. First, he did this in Mecca, but there were problems that obliged him to move to Medina, where he began to organize the life of the city. He needed to solve problems regarding property, family relations, economics, wars, and ethical prescriptions. Each time he thought he received from God the solution to these problems, he transmitted it under the form of qur'ānic verses. At the same time, he became increasingly affirmed as a political leader.

Needing money and wanting to expand his power, he organized raids against other Arab tribes. He reached agreements with different tribes and became stronger and richer. In the end, he challenged Mecca and conquered the entire Arabic peninsula for himself, imposing his vision of life, of God, and of relationships with others, which he named Islam. In my opinion, all this does not make him a prophet. In some respects, he reminds us of biblical figures such as Moses or Joshua; in some aspects of the first period in Mecca, he reminds us of the prophet Amos in his plea for social justice. But this does not make him a figure worthy of being considered a prophet, especially if I consider the moral and spiritual level of his teaching as compared to that of Christianity. I wonder how God, after sending Christ to preach the beatitudes and call for love of neighbor, could

"Teologia coranica di Cristo" [The Qur'ānic Theology of Christ], *La Civiltà Cattolica* 134, no. 3192 (1983): 556–64.

send someone with whom mankind basically takes a step backward by reintroducing the ancient *lex talionis* (an eye for an eye and a tooth for a tooth).

And to those who answer that Muhammad was a prophet specifically sent to Arabs, that statement is contradicted by Muslims themselves, who say that Muhammad is the prophet for all the peoples. It is true that, in his time, Muhammad made the polytheist Arabs (that is, those who were neither Jews nor Christians) advance as far as some pre-Islamic habits are concerned. But it is also true that, in some respects, he made them take a step backward by promoting the idea of religion linked with war and the idea of women's subservience to males in marriage. In general, Muhammad's divine revelations were contingent with the Arab society in which he lived.

From a Christian point of view, there is neither prophecy after John the Baptist nor revelation after Christ. I know that some Christian theologians propose that Muhammad be considered a prophet because, thanks to his preaching, more than one billion people profess monotheism. In my opinion, this proposal is not very convincing: having many followers can be meritorious for a person, but this does not make him a prophet. With this I have no intention of offending Muslims but only of making a reasonable observation. I also point to the fact that no official text of the Catholic Church ever recognized Muhammad as a prophet.

C. No to a Masquerade, Yes to the Search for Truth

101.   *What do you consider the value and the limits of dialogue between Christians and Muslims? It is a disputed and a controversial matter that is interpreted very differently by each group.*

*What is the most authentic and realistic Christian position for an
encounter with Muslims?*

Dialogue is far more than a specific activity reserved to theologians, or a luxury for a few intellectuals. It is a challenge
that millions of Christians and Muslims confront daily in
Europe. These meetings, whether in schools, workplaces,
neighborhoods, or apartment buildings, present the ground
for authentic communication, for identifying differences as
well as for exchanging a reciprocal heritage, and for learning what each group considers important for itself and others.

The preliminary condition for a dialogue is the presence
of two distinct voices. Each expression of a subject draws
from a well-defined face and identity. Today, especially on
the Christian side, it is a time of masking one's face and
cultural heritage in order to engage the other person. This
is dialogue of the lowest common denominator, of so-called
common values searched for at all costs as a starting point
instead of being arrived at as the possible result of a common journey.

This position is often motivated by good intentions and
by an authentic desire for encounter, but it does not lead
anyone very far. It neither helps us understand each other
more nor forms the conditions for a better coexistence.
Saying what the other likes to hear belongs more to diplomacy. If I were to look only at what is held in common,
I risk thinking that my interlocutor and I share similar ideas
with only the smallest and most insignificant differences.
However, the day in which one of the two discovers that
this is not the case, they could both lose trust in what
they had already said and accomplished up to that moment:
it would be like waking up from a beautiful dream and
suddenly discovering that reality is completely different.
Authentic dialogue requires love for the truth at all costs

and respect for the other in his integrity. It is not minimalist but rigorous.

If the first required condition of both the interlocutors is self-awareness, that is, the knowledge of one's own identity, the second condition must be the desire to inform the other person about one's position in its entirety (not avoiding the parts that will disturb the other or that generate questions) and to learn the position of the other one in its complexity, in order to discern and understand who is actually in front of him.

For Christians, this means speaking about the central tenets of their faith, such as the Incarnation, the death, and the Resurrection of Jesus, who is true man and true God, and the trinitarian dimension of God. It also means not to remain content with a common proclamation of monotheism, which is a very important dimension. It means not stopping in admiration of the fact that the Qur'ān mentions Jesus. The reality is that Jesus' role in the Qur'ān is reduced to being only a great prophet, while the Qur'ān ignores his most important work of being the way of salvation for all humanity.

Christians must never forget that presenting only a part of our faith or diminishing it for fear of offending, disappointing, or causing scandal does nothing more than confirm the Muslim interlocutors in their conviction (very widespread in Muslim countries and also present in the immigrant communities) that the Christian is a believer who has not reached the fullness of the truth, revealed in the Qur'ān. When I go to England, I am always struck by the large inscription on the wall of the Birmingham mosque that is visible from the highway to the airport: "Read the Qur'ān, the Last Testament."

Similarly ambiguous, and often detrimental for reciprocal understanding, are some practical behaviors adopted in the past years, almost always in good faith but with a great naiveté or with little knowledge of what was being done. In the name of solidarity, of brotherhood, or of "faith in the only God", parish buildings and even churches have been granted to the Muslim communities for their prayer, forgetting that for the followers of Muhammad this can mean not so much a favor but a capitulation, a sort of abdication of one's own faith and an implicit acknowledgment of the superiority of Islam. Nor ought we forget that, according to Muslim thought, a place that has been made holy to Islam can no longer be deconsecrated, and it is considered, even if in an implicit way and without any juridical formalization, as an Islamic property.

102.   *It is often stated that Christians and Muslims can collaborate in many fields, as in the promotion of peace and the defense of life (abortion, euthanasia, genetic manipulation), and in general on issues related to the so-called common values. But what is the authentic foundation for the dialogue? Is it an ethical foundation, or is there anything more radical on which it can be based at the anthropological level?*

For the Christian, reason is a given belonging to human nature that urges man to wonder about the meaning and the ultimate implications of his existence and that of the whole universe, which makes him realize the existence of the Mystery of God, who manifests himself in revelation. In this perspective, opened by Christianity, there is a starting point that is common for each person, a datum of nature that is developed and brought to fulfillment by the encounter with the ultimate meaning of reality, which is possible for everyone. In this sense, the notion of *natural law* represents a common ground between the believer and the secular, and it allows the acknowledgment of universal rights.

In the biblical vision, every person, not just the "believer", is created in God's image.[45] Consequently, every human being can find this divine "image", which can be a common value for each person, if he tries to deepen his consciousness of the meaning of life.

The Muslim, however, considers it inconceivable to speak of natural law apart from the religious law (*sharī'a*) given by God to man, being persuaded that there is no universal given that is not already included in the Islamic conception of life. While in Christianity one starts from reason and arrives at revelation, in the classic Islamic conception revelation comes before reason and prevails upon it, engulfs it. In Arabic, Islam is defined as *dīn al-fiṭra*, the natural religion of man.

It is interesting to observe that, for a long time, many Muslims attached to natural law a dignity of its own and autonomy from the religious law, even if this does not belong to the classic tradition. This fact is very important because it can both contribute to the evolution of Islamic thought and allow the acknowledgment of fundamental rights to those who are not Muslims.

The role of Christians here is fundamental because they can help further this discernment, perhaps by finding inspiration in those values that are defined and practiced as "common values". To be sure, these values are not the foundation of the dialogue, but they represent the historical opportunity for Christians and Muslims to meet and to find a common ground that the faithful of the two religions can share, for which they can fight, even if they have taken different logical and anthropological paths.

---

[45] This is absolutely denied by Islam. Many Muslim scholars think that one of Muhammad's *ḥadīth*, "God created man in his image", is the counterpart of the biblical verse in Genesis 2. In reality, the meaning of the adjective "his" in Islam is "in the image of man", while in the biblical text it is "in the image of God", as it is made clear in the rest of the verse.

The basis for the dialogue is not a set of theoretical statements or a series of values but the common human condition that implies openness to the Mystery, to the religious dimension of life. It would be wrong, in the name of the existing unshakable differences, to deny the possibility of common ground and of agreements on some specific issues, even if we must be aware that we may arrive at some crucial point where, after walking a part of the road together, the two paths separate again. For example, regarding the problem of equality between men and women, Christians acknowledge equality between men and women based on the validity of the natural law, while Muslims state the supremacy of the religious law, which denies this equality.

103.   *There are some aspects of the two religions that seem to have great similarity, such as the conception of God as merciful, the belonging to the religions of the Book, and the common Abrahamitic tradition. Can this be built upon?*

The road of authentic dialogue is a path made of level plains and very rough climbs, and we need good training for navigating it. For example, even behind identical or similar expressions, there can be totally different meanings that are important to learn in order to deepen one's knowledge of the truth, not for any desire to emphasize the distinctions. The sentence "God is merciful" for a Muslim means that God, the All Powerful, the transcendent, can bend down to man with mercy or deny his mercy to whomever he wishes. This is very different from the idea of the merciful God that we find in the Old and New Testaments. There God's mercy is like that of a parent for his child. For the Christian, in fact, God is the most authentic expression of love and the source of mercy that a father and a mother have toward their children. This conception is at the basis of all of the New Testament; it belongs to the essence of faith and is the beginning of the most common Christian prayer, the Our Father. And it is not by chance that among the ninety-nine names of God that the Muslim tradition draws from the Qur'ān, there is not the appellation "Father", being an attribute incompatible with the qur'ānic God and denied by the Qur'ān itself.

However, the word *rahm*, meaning "the womb", derives from the same Arabic root as the words "clement" and "merciful" (*rahmān* and *rahīm*). This means that the Arabic language could have suggested the "motherly" notion of God. However, this tradition was not developed by classic Islam, even though some mystics considered it. This point could represent an open door for the deepening of the concept of God common to Jews, Christians, and Muslims.

104. *Another example of analogies between Islam and Christianity is that both are considered "religions of the Book". Can this idea be used to further interreligious dialogue?*

The expression "people of the Book" is typically qur'ānic. With it, the Qur'ān defines Jews and Christians. The reason is that, in the Arab environment known by Muhammad, the only peoples who had a revealed book were Jews and Christians. Muslims did not have a holy book until two decades after Muhammad's death. Therefore, from the Muslim perspective, at the time Muhammad's third successor, khalif 'Uthmān, issued the Qur'ān is the first moment the three monotheistic religions can be called "religions of the Book".

This expression is ambiguous, even from a Christian perspective, for two reasons. First, it means implicitly acknowledging the Qur'ān as a book revealed by God to Muhammad, and this has never been acknowledged in Christianity and cannot be theologically justified.[46] Second, while for Muslims the divine revelation was announced once and for all time and in an accomplished way to humanity through the book of the Qur'ān, whose content directly descended from heaven, Christianity cannot be defined as being founded on a book, even if this book is revealed, and it cannot be "reduced" to the Holy Scriptures. In fact, the foundation of Christianity is not a book but an event: the Incarnation of God, who became man in the Person of Jesus Christ. The sign par excellence of the Christian faith is the Cross, on which Jesus sacrificed himself for love of man and for the salvation of all mankind.

It is not by chance that, from the beginning, the Eastern Christian communities venerated icons representing the Virgin Mary with Jesus, and not an icon of the Gospel or the Bible. And when in the liturgy the Gospel is taken in procession and incensed, it is because the Gospel revealed Christ to us. At the beginning of the second century, Ignatius of Antioch, in his Letter to the Philadelphians, is unequivocal: "My treasure is Jesus Christ, my irremovable archives are his cross, his death and resurrection and the faith that comes from him."

105.   *One last element of similarity that is often mentioned is that Muslims and Christians (as well as Jews) belong to the*

---

[46] Cf. Samir Khalil Samir, "Le Coran est-il révélé? Muhammad est-il prophète? Un point de vue chrétien" ["Is the Qur'ān Revealed? Is Muhammad a Prophet? A Christian Point of View"], in *Notre apostolat dans le monde musulman: Fatqā (Libano) 26 luglio–2 agosto 1999*, in Rencontre Vincentienne (Rome: Congrégation de la Mission, 2000), 292–299.

common Abrahamitic tradition. Is this possibly a starting point from where advancements in religious dialogue can be made?

The figure of Abraham is a classical issue of interreligious dialogue.[47] It is true that the three religions are called, a bit unduly, "Abrahamitic" because all acknowledge Abraham as their father. Some authors underline the ambiguity of the term, claiming that it could be a sort of homonym.[48] It is certain that these three religions refer to Abraham as the perfect example of the believer who completely relied on God, to the point of being ready to sacrifice his own son.

The Old Testament already speaks of Abraham as the father of a multitude of peoples:

> Behold, my covenant is with you, and you shall be the father of a multitude of nations. No longer shall your name be Abram, but your name shall be Abraham; for I have made you the father of a multitude of nations. I will make you exceedingly fruitful; and I will make nations of you, and kings shall come forth from you. And I will establish my covenant between me and you and your descendants after you throughout their generations for an everlasting covenant, to be God to you and to your descendants after you.[49]

The theme is expressed by different authors in the New Testament, especially by Paul, particularly in the Letters to the Romans and to the Galatians.

[47] See, for example, Eugène Tissérant, *Abraham père des croyants* [Abraham, the Father of the Believers] (Paris: Cerf, 1952).

[48] See, for example, Alain Besançon, *Trois tentations dans l'Église* [Three Temptations in the Church] (Paris: Calman-Lévy, 1996), 174–76; and Antoine Moussali, *La croix et le croissant: Le christianisme face à l'Islam* [The Cross and the Crescent: Christianity Confronted with Islam] (Paris: Editions de Paris, 1998), 51–56.

[49] Gen 17:4–7.

The Qur'ān takes the image of Abraham as the spiritual guide of humanity: "When his Lord put Abraham to the proof by enjoining on him certain commandments and Abraham fulfilled them, He said: 'I have appointed you a leader of mankind.' "[50] The Qur'ān, however, contests the Jewish and Christian claim of the figure of Abraham and reverses the claim in favor of Islam. The Qur'ān tells both Jews and Christians that Abraham is neither a Christian nor a Jew but a Muslim. It states, "They [Jews and Christians] say: 'Accept the Jewish or the Christian faith and you shall be rightly guided'. [And God answers to Muhammad] Say: 'By no means! We believe in the faith of Abraham, the upright one. He was no idolater.' "[51] And in another passage: "People of the Book, why do you argue about Abraham when both the Torah and the Gospel were not revealed until after him? Have you no sense? ... Abraham was neither Jew nor Christian. He was an upright man, one who submitted to God. He was no idolater. Surely the men who are nearest to Abraham are those who follow him, this Prophet, and the true believers. God is the guardian of the faithful."[52]

Christianity and Islam view Abraham from two very different perspectives. In Islam, Abraham is the witness of the most radical monotheism, and like the other biblical figures, he is the model of perfect submission to God. The notion of the promise or covenant with Abraham, like that of the "history of salvation", which is common to Judaism and Christianity, is practically absent in Islam.[53]

Therefore, the Second Vatican Council, in the dogmatic constitution *Lumen gentium* states: "The plan of

[50] The Cow, sura 2:124.

[51] Ibid., 2:135.

[52] The 'Imrāns, sura 3:65–68.

[53] Even though we can find traces of it, as for example ibid. 3:33. See also the text used in the Council, in the declaration *Nostra aetate*, 3

salvation also includes those who acknowledge the Creator, in the first place, amongst whom are the Moslems, these profess to hold the faith of Abraham, and together with us, they adore the one, merciful God, mankind's judge in the last day." [54] The first drafting of this text said: "The sons of Ishmael who, professing Abraham as a father, also believe in the God of Abraham." The final version does not say anything about the relation between Muslims and Abraham, but it states only that Muslims profess "to hold the faith of Abraham." [55]

106. *For years, representatives of the Catholic hierarchy have tried to revive dialogue with their Muslim peers. Pope John Paul II led the way in this difficult task, and he was criticized by those who feared a watering down of the Church teaching. What was the position of John Paul II on interreligious dialogue?*

I am convinced that Pope John Paul II was the most significant expression of the Christian attempt to realize an authentic dialogue. He supported the building of bridges and of opportunities for encounters between Christians and Muslims. After the terrorist attack on the World Trade Center "Twin Towers" in New York City and during the war in Afghanistan, he strongly opposed the idea of a clash of civilizations or religions. A significant testimony of this attitude was the invitation addressed to Catholics for a day of fasting on December 14, 2001 (which coincided with the last day of Ramaḍān), and the meeting between the representatives of religions in Assisi on January 24, 2002.

[54] The Second Vatican Council, *Lumen gentium*, no. 16.
[55] The same text has been used in the *Catechism of the Catholic Church*, no. 841.

John Paul II very often spoke against the exploitation of religious faith for political or military goals, such as those hidden in some Muslim calls for war against the West, as well as in the Western efforts to counter Islamic terrorism. He was aware that a part of Islam, probably a minority but nevertheless capable of influencing the community, fuels conflicts and uses religious code words to try to consolidate the Muslim world by exploiting tragic situations, such as the Palestinian problem. He also knew that the polarization of the positions would be a catastrophe not only for the Christian minorities living in Islamic countries but also for all of humanity, which could be obliged to face one billion Muslims united by certain code words.

While he spoke about the need for a dialogue between different religions, John Paul II never failed to emphasize the necessity of promoting respect for human rights, among which he put in first place that of religious freedom, which by implication includes the freedom to profess one's own faith or to convert to another one: freedoms that are still to be recognized in many Islamic countries.

John Paul II's position revealed itself to be an admirable synthesis between the reaffirmation of the Christian faith and the concern that it be allowed to be practiced everywhere. At the meeting with religious leaders of all faiths in Assisi, he said of religious dialogue that "it does not push for opposition and even less the contempt for the other; rather, it allows for a constructive dialogue where each person, without indulging in relativism or syncretism, acquires a deeper conscience about the duty of witnessing and announcing."

107.   *Through the many initiatives of voluntary service groups, thousands of Catholics have been working for years on the front line in the reception of immigrants, many of whom are Muslim.*

What are the conditions that allow these daily meetings also to become opportunities for dialogue?

What Catholic volunteers do in Italy from the point of view of giving assistance to immigrants deserves respect and admiration for their generosity and dedication provided. On many occasions, however, I have noticed the volunteers exhibit a certain difficulty in expressing the motives for such generosity or in explaining their actions as an expression of their Christian love and faith. At the same time, they seem embarrassed, or reserved, when caring for the Muslim immigrants. I have met Christian volunteers in the shelters and soup kitchens who forwent making the sign of the cross before meals as a "sign of respect" for the religious feelings of the Muslims hosted there. It seems to me that their sign of respect is a mistake because it renounces the true reasons for their activity and for the work accomplished. Why would a Christian organize a dining room for the poor and for immigrants, whatever their faith, if not to fulfill the duty of Christian charity? Christians never need to be ashamed of witnessing their faith to all the people they encounter. If this were not so, the shelters and pantries supported by the Church would run the risk of becoming "solidarity supermarkets", carrying out a certainly praiseworthy activity but betraying their true motive of giving visible Christian testimony.

It is not a matter of proselytism but of authenticity, of the ability to express the truth about ourselves in what we do. It would certainly be wrong to *condition* the bread that we offer to Muslim immigrants with conversion to Christianity; this would be an unacceptable act of proselytism. What is needed is authenticity, the simple witnessing of the Christian faith that moves the volunteers and educates them to help everybody without any religious, ideological, or political position, to share with those in need in order to share the sense of life. We need to examine seriously the ways in which these activities are organized and proposed, so that they may become pedagogical actions both for those Christians who accomplish them and for those members of other faiths who benefit from them.

108.   *Can the migratory experience contribute to modifying the traditional vision and prejudices of Muslims toward Christianity and Christians?*

A widespread misconception in Islamic countries is that the Christian is a believer who did not reach the fullness of faith, which can be achieved only through adherence to qur'ānic teachings. Christians have to overcome stereotypic identification of Muslims that developed over centuries. Muslim immigration to Europe is a great chance to help demystify some commonplace fears and prejudices and foster better understanding of Christianity and of Christians.

In Europe, the Muslim immigrant can realize that there are other religious experiences, apart from that of Islam, with which it is possible to coexist in a milieu of freedom and pluralism. A maturation of different potentials can take place, including living as believers even without the "guarantees" offered by a confessional state. Muslims can learn that politics can be separated from religion, that the secular can serve the common good, that reason is not the enemy but a friend of faith, and that modernity is a historical opportunity to measure the truth of one's faith in the world. It is wrong to identify Christianity with the West, even if the Christian faith is one of the most important foundational elements of the West.

In this context, the testimony Christians are required to give is decisive. Some aspects of modern-day Western life, such as widespread ethical relativism, a mistaken conception of freedom that is confused with the possibility of doing whatever one wants without any moral reference, and the commercialization of the human body, confirm Muslims in their judgment of Western society as corrupt and decadent.

I believe that these aspects of Western culture must be addressed with far more criticism on the part of Christians because they are significant indicators of a society that removed God from its reference points and that considers religion as an ornament to be displayed in a sort of "parlor room of values": something interesting—perhaps also original—but irrelevant to one's life. When Muslims criticize Western society for its dissolute habits and consider it a society that renounced God, they indirectly urge Christians to question themselves on the meaning of their own presence in this society, on the worth of their testimony, and on the weight of faith in the environment in which they live.

Immigration can represent for Christians a challenge to overcome centuries of nonaction. In past centuries, many European Christian missionaries went to Muslim countries. Their preaching, however, was forbidden or substantially neutralized by the strong cultural and social pressure of Islam, and this prevented millions of Muslims from ever knowing of Christianity, and I mean knowing of it, not converting to it. Today, in an opposite demographic movement, millions of Muslims come to the Europe from which the Christian missionaries left. Yet Muslims find a society where Christianity is absent or approaching extinction. Many Muslim friends who came to Europe express their disappointment at the fact that they thought they would find Christianity firmly established in the West and the society permeated by Christian values and ideals, but they found only light traces of it.

Perhaps the presence of so many Muslims can act as a stimulus to reawaken Christians from their dormant faith practices. The Muslim presence in Europe, like that of the Christian immigrants coming from the Third World (who often give a more dynamic witness to their faith), can encourage Western Christians to spiritual renewal.

109.   *Is the idea of dialogue foreign to the Muslim mentality? It seems that efforts at dialogue always start on the Christian side, and the result is a conversation with deaf people. What would you answer to those who consider the efforts accomplished in these past years as naïve and useless?*

The efforts connected to the culture of dialogue were almost always begun by Christians, even though in the last decades there have been some initial openings by the Muslim world. The Muslim-Christian encounter promoted by CERES (Centre d'Études et de Recherches Économiques et Sociales) and by the Āl al-Bayt Foundation (funded by Prince Ḥassan, the brother of the late King Ḥussein of Jordan) was a series of bilateral meetings with the participation of representatives of the Islamic al-Azhar University, both in the Vatican and in Cairo. There is also the activity of small but meaningful groups in Lebanon. Some Muslim intellectuals publicly acknowledged that in their world there is a slowness to engage the West in dialogue that must be overcome, and while there is a sizable group of Christian experts on Islam, there are very few Muslim experts on Christianity. Moreover, the Islamic editorial treatment of Christianity is normally polemic in form and quite aggressive or apologetic, with the declared or implicit goal of defending Islam from "Western accusations". Some Muslim intellectuals started a careful consideration of Christianity with a dialogical attitude, but they could not continue for lack of any real current dialogue with the West at the moment.

Muslims believe that Islam is the ultimate and definitive revealed religion. They believe that the Qur'ān includes true Judaism and authentic Christianity. Muslims are convinced that Jews and Christians falsified their own Scriptures. For Muslim believers who believe that they already have the full truth, there is very little to gain or to learn through interreligious dialogue. It is obvious that this attitude creates a blockade to any possibility of developing a real dialogue with Western Christians. However, the reasons for a truthful encounter remain valid. We must pray that reason will prevail in this matter. As John Paul II said in Assisi, to pray "does not mean to escape from history and from the problems that it brings along. On the contrary, it means to choose to face reality not by ourselves but with the strength that comes from on high, the strength of Truth and Love whose ultimate source is God."

110.   *The Christian Arabs have a thirteen-century history of coexistence with Islam. What are the insights that can be derived from their experience?*

First, contrary to what many people think, both in the West and in the East, "Arab" is not synonymous with "Muslim". The second chapter of Saint Luke's Acts of the Apostles reminds us that, on the day of Pentecost, among the neophytes converted to Christianity, there were also some Arabs. Today there are more than twelve million Christian Arabs. The Arabs were not born with Muhammad. Before the birth of Islam, in the Arabic peninsula, there lived tribes of Arab-Jews, Arab-Christians, and Arab-pagans. After Muhammad's preaching and the Muslim expansion in the Middle East (A.D. 636–642), the non-Arab Christians of that area were gradually Arabized and forced to live with Muslims under the jurisdiction of Islam as protected people.[56]

Over the centuries, there were many positive experiences of encounter and exchange between Muslims and Christians at a personal level, based on the fact that both sides consider fundamental the transcendental dimension of life and the absoluteness of certain values. Real problems were raised by the Christian encounter with Islam as a sociopolitical system, which followed the politicization of religion. Since then there has been a tendency in the Muslim tradition of imposing its domination. This tendency derives from the Muslim conviction that they have a monopoly on the truth and that the Qur'ān is the perfect and ultimate revelation.

For centuries, Christian Arabs have been constantly reminded by Muslims of the absolute priority to acknowledge God in every aspect and moment of daily life. I have a personal experience of the Muslim sense of responsibility to acknowledge God that affected me very deeply. While I was in Cairo, on a Friday, I entered a barbershop shortly before noon. The owner politely told me, "In a few minutes, there is the ritual prayer, and I shall stop my work; I would advise you to go to the Christian hairdresser, a few meters away." His sincerity and honesty persuaded me to remain in his shop waiting until the end of the ritual prayer. He was a true believer. He was ready to lose a customer in order not to avoid an act of faith. Unfortunately, this priority for Muslims to acknowledge God can easily degenerate both into fanaticism and into neglecting one's responsibilities toward society. Christian Arabs have learned to appreciate both the positive and the negative aspects of coexistence, avoiding both the temptation of naïve unreserved acceptance and that of

---

[56] See question 37, p. 91 above.

prejudicial opposition and systematic rejection of the other tradition.

111.   *Can one then speak of a sort of historical vocation of the Christian Arabs to act as the bridge between two civilizations that are, simultaneously, both far and near from the other?*

As a matter of fact, Christian Arabs can help Western Christians both to understand Islam in all its dimensions and how to coexist with it. They need only communicate the fruits of their millenary experience. Indeed, Christian Arabs can be a bridge because they are different from Westerners insofar as they are Arab. They are different from Muslims because they are Christians. They are considered foreigners by both worlds, even though they deeply belong to each of them. This has been at times a very uncomfortable and problematic position. Yet it is the *sine qua non* condition actually to serve as an interreligious and intercultural bridge between East and West. Historically, it is a true vocation by virtue of their Christian baptism to be ministers of reconciliation in the world. This means to be united to Jesus on the Cross, horizontally reconciling humanity with itself and vertically reconciling humanity with God.

APPENDICES

Appendix A. Chronology of Islam

Muhammad

ca. 570	Muhammad's birth, shortly after his father's death.
577	Death of Muhammad's mother, Amīna. Muhammad is first raised by his grandfather, then by his uncle.
ca. 591	Muhammad goes into service with Khadīja as a caravaneer. He marries her five years later.
610	Muhammad receives the verses of the Qur'ān. For three years, Muhammad's preaching is secret.
613	Public preaching in Mecca.
615	The hostility of the Quraysh tribe causes the exodus of some Muslims to Ethiopia.
622	Muhammad's emigration (Hegira) to Yathrib (Medina).
624	Muslim victory over Mecca in the battle of Badr.
628	Muslim conquest of the Jewish oasis of Khaybar.
630	Muhammad's triumphal entry into Mecca.
632	Muhammad dies in Medina.

Khalifate

632–633	War against the "apostates".
634	The military campaign against the Byzantine and Persian empires begins.
636	The Battle of Yarmūk: the Byzantines lose Syria.
639–642	The conquest of Egypt.

653	The fixing of the text of the Qur'ān under khalif 'Uthmān.
656	'Alī, Muhammad's cousin and son-in-law, is elected fourth khalif.
656–657	Civil war between 'Alī and 'Aisha, Muhammad's widow: Muslims divide into Sunni, Shiite, and Kharijites factions.
660	Mo'āwiya proclaims himself khalif in Damascus. The Umayyad dynasty begins.
668–673	First siege of Constantinople.
670	Muslim expansion in North Africa.
680	Slaughter of Hussein, 'Alī's son, in Karbala. The breach between Sunni and Shiite widens.
711	Crossing of the Strait of Gibraltar. Fall of the Visigothic reign.
713	The eastern expansion reaches the delta of the Indus River.
732	Muslim expansion into Europe stopped by Charles Martel at the Battle of Poitiers.
750	The Umayyad dynasty collapses (except in Andalusia). The Abbasid dynasty begins.
786–809	Khalifate of Hārūn al-Rashīd. Maximum height of glory of the Muslim empire.
827–902	Arab conquest of Sicily.
954	Expansion of Ishmaelite Islam in India.
969	Fatimid conquest of Egypt and foundation of Cairo and of al-Azhar mosque.
ca. 1000	First conversions of black African leaders.
1000–1021	Rule of the Fatimid khalif al-Hākim: worsening of the measures against Christians.
11th century	Conversion to Islam of the African kingdom of Ghana.
1061–1092	Conquered by Normans, the Arabs leave Sicily.

1071	The victory of the Seljuks over the Byzantines opens Asia Minor to Turkish tribes.
1076	The Seljuks take Damascus from the Fatimids.
1099	The Christian Crusaders occupy Jerusalem.
1187	Saladin's victory at Hattīn.
13th century	Expansion of Islam into Bengal following the conversion of Buddhists and Hindus.
1236	Conquest of Cordova by Ferdinand III of Castile.
1258	Conquest of Baghdad by the Mongolians. End of Abbasid khalifate.
1317	First Muslim king sits on the throne of Dongola, once a Christian Nubian kingdom.
Mid-15th century	Settlement of Islam on the island of Java.
1453	Conquest of Constantinople by Ottoman Turks.
1475	Introduction of Islam in the Philippines.
1492	The Spanish *Reconquista* ends with the capitulation of Granada.
16th century	Destruction of the last Nubian Christian state.
1506	*Jihād* of the al-Ghazi *imām* against Christians in Ethiopia.
1516	Victory of the Ottomans against the Mamelukes and occupation of Syria.
1526	Battle of Mohács. Hungary falls under the Ottoman Empire.
1526–1858	Reign of the Moghul dynasty in India.
1529	Siege of Vienna by the Ottomans.
1571	Defeat of the Ottoman fleet in the battle of Lepanto.
1798–1801	Campaign of Napoleon Bonaparte's army in Egypt.
1865–1885	Russian conquest of the Islamic territories in Central Asia.

1918	The Ottoman Empire is defeated in World War I.
1924	Abolition of the khalifate by Mustafa Kemal.
2000	Beginning of War against the Taliban in Afghanistan.
2003	Invasion of Iraq leading to the fall from power of Saddam Hussein. Process to institute a democratic government begun.

Contemporary Age

1932	The kingdom of Saudi Arabia is born.
1947	Establishment of a state for Indian Muslims: Pakistan.
1948	Creation of the state of Israel; the beginning of the Palestinian diaspora.
1962	Independence of Algeria at the end of a long conflict with French colonial domination.
1967–1970	Civil war in Biafra opposes Christians and Nigerian Muslims.
1969	Establishment of the Conference of Islamic Organizations.
1979	The Islamic revolution of Khomeini prevails in Iran.
1979–1989	The *mujāhidīn* fight against the Soviet Union army, which occupies Afghanistan.
1980–1988	Iran-Iraq war. Mediation efforts by the Islamic countries prove useless.
1983	Proclamation of *sharīʿa* in Sudan. An insurrection in the southern part of the country erupts.
1987	After years of conflict led by the Moro (Moor) National Liberation Front, an agreement with the Philippine government is signed.
1990	Iraq invades Kuwait. American troops are sent to the Gulf region.
1991	Gulf War: Conference of Madrid held between Arabs and Israelis.

1992	Violent actions by Islamic groups start in Algeria.
1993	Oslo Agreements between Israel and Arafat's Palestinian Liberation Organization opposed by radical groups.
1996	Afghan Talibans enter Kabul.
1999–2002	Many states of the Nigerian federation proclaim *sharī'a*.
2000	The second Palestinian *Intifada* breaks out.
2001	Terrorist attacks in New York and Washington. The head of al-Qā'ida, Bin Lādin, repeatedly praises the attackers and launches *jihād* against the West. International diplomatic and military offensive launched against terrorism.

Appendix B. Muslims in the European Union

Nation	Population (millions)	Muslims (millions)	Percentage
Older Member States			
France	60.4	5	8.3
Germany	82	3.5	4.3
United Kingdom	58.6	1.6	2.7
Italy	57.6	1	1.8
Spain	39.4	1	2.4
Netherlands	15.8	1	6.3
Belgium	10.2	0.4	3.9
Sweden	8.9	0.4	4.4
Austria	8.1	0.35	4.4
Switzerland	7.2	0.31	4.3
Denmark	5.3	0.27	5
Norway	4.6	0.08	1.8
	358.1	15.3	4.3
Newer Member States and Accession States through 2007–2008			
Poland	38.7	0	
Portugal	10.8	0	
Greece	10.6	0.14	1.3
Czech Republic	10.3	0	
Hungary	10.1	0	
Slovakia	5.4	0	
Finland	5.2	0	

(*continued*)

Ireland	3.7	0	
Lithuania	3.7	0	
Latvia	2.4	0	
Slovenia	2	0.05	
Estonia	1.4	0	
Cyprus	0.9	0.16	18
Malta	0.4	0	
Luxembourg	0.4	?	
Romania	22.3	0.2	0.8
Bulgaria	7.5	0.9	12.2
	135.8	1.45	1.1

Membership currently under negotiation, or candidate countries (excluding Turkey)

Croatia	4.5	0.2	4.4
Macedonia	2.1	0.6	17
Albania	3.6	2.5	70
Serbia and Montenegro	10.8	2.2	19
Bosnia and Herzegovina	4.1	1.6	40
	25.1	7.1	28.2
EUROPEAN TOTALS	**521**	**23.8**	**4.6**
Turkey	70	70	99.9

SOURCE: *CIA Factbook*, available online at www.cia.gov/library/publications/the-world-factbook/

According to the same source, in 2008 Muslims are 0.6% of the population of the United States. — ED.

Appendix C. Islam in Italy

How Many Muslims Are in Italy?[1]

When one has to "measure" religious identity, statistics can help, but they are never decisive. The quantification of Italian Islam that we propose derives from the sum of two realities: that of *immigrants*, which includes both the legal and the illegal ones, and that of *Italians*, which counts those foreigners who have acquired Italian citizenship and Italians who have converted to Islam.

For foreigners, one refers to the percentage of Muslims compared to the total population registered in the immigrants' countries of origin, and that is "projected" onto the Italian context as well. On the basis of this criterion, the 2001 edition of the Immigration Statistical Report published by Caritas (this report is generally considered the most authoritative tool in this field because it uses data collected by the Ministry of the Interior) calculates 613,000 foreign Muslims residing in Italy at the end of 2000. The figure represents 36.8 percent of the total foreign population. Three other categories of people must be added: those illegal immigrants who live in a clandestine situation, those who came from abroad but have obtained Italian citizenship, and those

[1] Although the present edition is intended for English-speaking readers, it was decided to retain the author's Appendix on Islam in Italy in order to give readers insight into the context in which the author was writing. — ED.

citizens of Italian origin who have converted to Islam. All three categories are difficult to quantify, so we can only estimate that approximately 700,000 Muslims lived in Italy in 2000.

Where Do the Muslims Come From?

The Muslim community in Italy is the most diversified in all of Europe when the geographical origins of its members are considered. Unlike in France, Germany, and Great Britain, where the dominant immigrant groups are Maghrebians, Turks, and Hindu Pakistanis, respectively, in Italy one meets Muslims from a great variety of ethnic and national backgrounds.

They come from Africa, especially Maghreb and Egypt; they come from eastern Europe, especially Albania; and some are of Asian origin. The most numerically significant are Moroccans, followed by Tunisians and Senegalese plus several other national groups. The Albanian community has undergone the greatest numerical increase, due to massive arrivals after the fall of the Communist regime and the economic–social collapse of the nation. This group increased from 2,000 officially registered Albanian immigrants in 1991 to 142,000 registered immigrants by the end of 2000.

The Family Dimension

Males make up the majority of the Muslim immigrant population in Italy, though there are differences inside the various communities. Women do not exceed 20 percent of immigrants from North Africa but comprise 30 percent of those from Albania. In the last few years, despite a severe reduction in legal entries for work-related reasons, family sponsorships of close relatives have significantly increased.

This trend happened in all the national communities with strong Islamic ties, which affirms that the process of stabilization is ongoing in Italy. Therefore, beyond the numbers, the importance of the family dimension in Italian Islam (and of the problems connected with it, including questions about marriages, about the education of children, about schools, and about the second generation) is increasing.

The Organizations

The majority of Muslims who live in Italy practice Islam at a personal level, in the family and in small communities. Because they come from such a wide variety of geographical origins and very different ethnic-national backgrounds, they do not favor blanket organizations. There is also a remarkable diversity in their doctrinal and spiritual affiliations. The majority are Sunni, and Shiites are a minority. Some Muslims are affiliated with confraternities, a mystic component of Islam, which are quite widespread. There are about ten of them, and the most important is the *Muridiya*, to which three quarters of the Senegalese community belong, while a minority of the same ethnic community adheres to the *Tijaniya* confraternity.

The most widespread and deep-rooted organization at the national level is the Union of Islamic Communities and Organizations in Italy (UCOII), founded in Ancona in 1990. It inherited the leadership of the Union of Muslim Students in Italy (USMI), which was founded in Perugia in 1971 and is connected with the international Muslim Brotherhood organization. The UCOII claims to be the umbrella organization that oversees approximately 70 Islamic centers and 120 places of worship in all the Italian regions. In 1992, it presented a request for the negotiation of an agreement with the Italian state. The UCOII can be described as the most public expression of the "*Islam of the mosques*", in which radical tendencies in support of the gradual Islamization of society coexist with neotraditionalist ideas that aim at creating a space in society where collective Muslim rights and constitutional guarantees are acknowledged. Recently, there has been an ongoing debate in Italy about the integration of Muslims into national society, that is, how Muslims can guarantee the protection of their religious identity in a manner compatible with Italian jurisprudence. The president of the UCOII is Muhammad Nour Dachan, who is of Syrian origin, and the general secretary is the Italian convert Hamza Roberto Piccardo.

The organization that best expresses the meaning of the "*Islam of the states*" is the *Islamic Cultural Center of Italy* (ICCI), founded in 1966. Its board of directors is formed by the ambassadors of Muslim countries (Sunni) to Italy or to the Vatican. The center is in charge of the mosque of Rome, inaugurated on June 21, 1995, and considered the largest in Europe. Its construction, which cost around 100 billion lira, was mainly financed by Saudi Arabia, which now pays a sizable portion of the operating costs. The center is the only Islamic organization in Italy that has obtained the status of a nonprofit organization (1974) from the state, and it owes its authority to its organic relation with the native countries of the Muslims living in Italy. For this very reason, it is questioned by those who reject any interference of foreign governments in affairs of the immigrants' communities. The Italian prime minister received a letter from the organization in 1993 that requested the opening of negotiations for an agreement.

The *World Muslim League–Italy* was formally founded in 1998. It is the Italian branch of the World Muslim League (*Rābitat al-ʿĀlam al-Islāmī*), which was founded in Mecca in 1962. It is one of the main Islamic international organizations.

The president of the Italian group is the Saudi Abdallah bin Saliḥ al-Obeid, a former general secretary of the World Muslim League; the vice president is a former Italian ambassador to Saudi Arabia, Mario Scialoja. In Italy, about twenty-five places of worship adhere to the "network" promoted and run by Hamza Massimiliano Boccolini, benefiting from the World Muslim League's material and legal assistance. The league defines itself as an organization dedicated to "spreading of the correct message of Islam, a religion of peace, tolerance and brotherhood. Its task is to oppose the political ideologies and currents which damage the image of Islam in the West." Its aim is to unify all Italian Muslims in order to negotiate an agreement with the Italian government.

The *Italian Islamic Religious Community* (Coreis) was founded in 1993 as the "International Association for Information on Islam". The charismatic figure ʿAbd al-Wāḥid Pallavicini, one of the first Italians converted to Islam (1951), was its founder. The organization is mainly constituted by converts who claim the role of guides and "scholars" for the community. It carries out vibrant cultural, editorial, and media activity both in Italy and abroad. It opposes any form of confessional exclusivity or ideological hegemony of Islamic origin and refuses to follow political currents in foreign states. It presented a formal request to negotiate an agreement with the Italian government in 1996.

The *Italian Muslim Association* (AMI) proposes a modern form of Sunni Islam in opposition to the most radical tendencies operating in Italy. In 1993, the AMI presented a draft for an agreement with the Italian state. AMI is directed by the Italian convert Massimo Abdul-Hadi Palazzi.

The *Islamic Cultural Institute* (ICI) was founded in 1998 following the split of the Islamic Center in Milan and Lombardy from the UCOII. The ICI is considered the gathering place of the most radical elements in the Muslim communities. As a result, it has often been the subject of judicial inquiries because of suspicions that it is involved in the Islamic terrorist networks operating at the international level. This is a charge repeatedly refuted by the president of the institute, Abdel-Hamid Shaari, a Libyan with Italian citizenship.

With the goal of amalgamating the multiple Islamic organizations operating in Italy and of giving birth to an organization that could negotiate an agreement with the Italian state, the *Islamic Counsel of Italy* was founded in 1998. It is composed of a board of ten members, all Italian citizens, representing the UCOII, the Islamic Cultural Center of Italy, the World Muslim League–Italy, and Coreis. However, the internal instability of the counsel, the vetoes by some of its members, and the external influences exercised by some states (particularly Saudi Arabia and Morocco) have thwarted the effort to establish a united representative group to advance the Muslim cause.

The majority of Muslims living in Italy do not feel they are or can be represented by any of the organizations mentioned above. They live their Islamic identity in an individual and informal manner. Various sources agree that only 5 percent of Muslims in Italy regularly attend the mosque for Friday prayer.

Glossary

Allāh
God. The word *Allāh* is a contraction of the Arab word *al-ilāh* (the god), meaning the God par excellence. Both Christians and Jews whose mother tongue is Arabic use this word for God. In Islam, Allah has ninety-nine divine names, such as the Merciful, the Sovereign, the Saint, the Watchful, etc.

āya
Divine sign. In Muslim usage, *āya* also refers to any single qur'ānic verse.

khalifate
The office of Muhammad's successor, as head of Islam. The English word "khalifate" derives from the Arabic word *khilāfa* (succession). The office of khalifate continued, almost uninterrupted, from the death of Muhammad in 632 to 1924, when it was abolished from the Turkish republic. Today, its reconstruction is considered necessary by many radical Muslim groups to liberate the world from the so-called *jāhiliyya*.

daʿwa
The call. It indicates the task of promulgating Islam through missionary activity.

dhimmī
Protected people. It refers to the people of the Book, which in Muslim understanding are Hebrew and Christian faithful, who have a sacred book. These people are under the protection (*dhimma*) of the Islamic state, under some precise conditions, particularly the payment of a per capita tax (levied on the individual), the

jizya. With the passing of time, the condition of *dhimmī* has become a synonym for "second-class citizens".

dīn wa dunya wa dawla

An expression meaning "religion, society, and state". It is a formula that describes Islam according to the classical Muslim conception as well as many modern interpretations; the three elements are considered inseparable.

fātiḥa

Opening. It refers to the first sura of the Qur'ān, used as ritual prayer by Muslims. It reads as follows: "In the name of God, the Compassionate, the Merciful. / Praise be to God, Lord of the Universe, / The Compassionate, the Merciful, / Sovereign of the Day of Judgment! You alone we worship, and to You alone we turn for help. / Guide us to the straight path, / The path of those whom You have favored, / Not of those who have incurred Your wrath, / Nor of those who have gone astray."

fatwā

A response or juridical religious decision on a matter given by a jurist regarding a precise request.

fiqh

The Muslim law. The Muslim texts gave rise to various interpretations by the different juridical schools. The specialist of *fiqh* is called a *faqīh* (plural, *fuqahā'*).

ḥadīth

Muhammad's sayings and deeds as reported and collected by his fellows or by their disciples. He who studies them is called *muḥaddith*. There are six large collections of *ḥadīth* considered authentic (*ṣaḥīḥ*).

ḥajj

The pilgrimage to Mecca. It is the fifth pillar of Islam; it has to be accomplished at least once in a lifetime, between the ninth and the thirteenth day of the month of Dhu-l-ḥijja, by those who have the possibility to do it. Every year, at least two million

Muslims take part in it, following a detailed ritual. Among the most important actions are the *ṭawāf*, which consists of walking around the Kaʿba seven times; the *saʿy*, or running between the two hills of Ṣafā and Marwa; the symbolic stoning of the devil near Minā; and the offering of an animal sacrifice. The ritual culminates in the prayer on Mount ʿArafat. When it is accomplished outside of the month of Dhu-l-hijja, the pilgrimage to Mecca is considered "small" and therefore called *ʿumra* (visit).

Hegira

Emigration (from the Arabic *Hijra*). It refers to Muhammad's flight from Mecca to Yathrib, a city later renamed Madīnat al-nabī (the city of the Prophet, or Medina). The event marks the beginning of the lunar calendar (A.D. 622).

ḥudūd

The plural form of *ḥadd* (limit). The word defines the qur'ānic "canonical" punishments, which are derived from the application of *sharīʿa*.

iʿjāz

Miracle. In Muslim tradition, it refers to the Qur'ān, whose literary style is considered "inimitable", thus proving the work's divine origin.

imām

A religious title that indicates the one who "sits in the front", one who guides the collective prayer in the mosque. According to the Shiites, the title was attributed to the twelve descendants of ʿAli, those who led the community one after the other, and therefore it is for only a privileged few, as it was for *imām* Khomeini.

Islam

Submission. The word derives from the verb *aslama*. For Muslims (the people subjected to God), Islam is man's "natural" and original religion. In this sense, in the Qur'ān, all the prophets sent by God are considered Muslims.

jāhiliyya
Literally, "ignorance". It indicates the Arabic pre-Islamic society, but today it indicates the society that does not know or does not apply Islam, that is, a barbarian or ignorant, pagan society.

jihād
To strive, to fight (from the Arabic root *j-h-d*). The context in which this word (masculine in Arabic) recurs in the Qur'ān is that of *jihād fī sabīl Allāh* (fight on the way to God), which Muslim exegetes understand as a synonym for holy war. The thesis, very widespread in the West, that it is necessary to distinguish between the "small *jihād*" (the holy war) and the "great *jihād*" (the ethical-spiritual effort against evil) is confirmed neither in the classical Islamic tradition nor in the theoretical elaboration of the Islamic groups that refer to *jihād*, while it is characteristic of the mystic currents.

Ka'ba
The cubic construction that is placed in the middle of the courtyard of the Great Mosque in Mecca, around which Muslims walk seven times, making the *ṭawāf* during the pilgrimage (see *ḥajj*, above). The Ka'ba contains the "black stone", a block of dark porphyry (perhaps a meteorite). According to the Muslim tradition, it is the place where Abraham erected an altar to God. For this reason, Muhammad preserved the construction, but he ordered the destruction of the symbols of the pre-Islamic divinities that had been erected around it.

kāfir
An unbeliever or polytheist, one who rejected faith (plural, *kuffār* or *kāfirūn*).

Khomeinist
Referring to groups that adopt Ayatollah Khomeini's Shiite "revolutionary" doctrine, particularly the thesis on the "government of the scholar" (*velayet-e-faqih*).

mosque
"Mosque" comes from the Arabic *masjid* (place of prostration). The mosque does not mean a "Muslim church", as it represents

not only a place of worship but also a center of cultural, social, and political assembly.

muezzin

In Arabic, *mu'adhdhin* (the one who performs the *adhān*, the call to prayer from the top of a minaret). The call starts by pronouncing *Allāh-u akbar* (God is the greatest) four times, followed by the *shahāda* (each sentence twice), then by the call itself: "Come to prayer, come to salvation" (each sentence twice), finishing with a new *Allāh-u akbar* (twice) and finally with "There is no god other than Allah."

muftī

The one who issues the *fatwa*. In many Muslim countries, the office of *muftī* indicates the highest religious charge of a state or a region.

mujāhidīn

The plural of *mujāhid* (fighter in the *jihād*).

Naṣāra

Nazarenes. The term is used in the Qur'ān and in Muslim tradition to indicate Christians.

pillars of the faith

They are five, compulsory for each Muslim upon reaching the age of puberty: the *shahāda* (the witnessing of the faith), the *ṣalāt* (the ritual prayer), the *zakāt* (the alms), the *ṣawm* (the fasting of Ramaḍān), and the *ḥajj* (the pilgrimage to Mecca).

qibla

The orientation of prayer, established by Muhammad, toward Mecca, following the Jewish practice of facing Jerusalem. All mosques are built respecting this orientation.

Qur'ān

The holy book of Muslims (from the Arabic *al-Qur'ān*, meaning "recitation" or "proclamation"). The name of the book derives from the first exhortation of the Archangel Gabriel to Muhammad: *Iqra'* (Read! Recite!). The Qur'ān is composed of 114 suras, or chapters, all of them organized according to their length except for the first, called *fātiḥa*.

ridda

Apostasy from Islam, also called *Irtidad*. The punishment for the *murtadd* (the apostate), at least in theory, is death.

ṣalāt

The ritual prayer. It consists of preestablished gestures and sentences. It can be communitarian (as in the mosque) or individual. It must be recited five times a day (dawn, midday, afternoon, sunset, and late evening) in the direction of Mecca, always in a state of "legal purity", that is, after practicing the necessary ablutions. It is the second pillar of Islam.

ṣawm

Fasting. It generally refers to the fast observed during the whole lunar month of Ramaḍān, which corresponds to the fourth pillar of the faith. It consists in the abstention from any food or beverage and from pleasures from dawn to sunset. It is compulsory for all Muslims from the age of puberty. Sick persons, travelers, and pregnant women are exempt. The fasting of a menstruating woman is not valid, and she is required to recover the lost days later on.

shahāda

The profession of faith in Allah and in his prophet. This first pillar of Islam consists in saying, "I witness that there is no god other than Allah and that Muhammad is Allah's messenger" (*ashhadu an lā ilāha illa Allāh wa anna Muhammad rasūl Allāh*). For a non-Muslim, it is sufficient to pronounce it to become Muslim.

sharīʿa

A common abbreviation of *sharīʿat Allāh* (the law of God). In the Qur'ān, it is always a law of divine origin, of a "way" that opposes the "passions of those who do not know". Today, its application, particularly in criminal law, is the main claim of the radical groups and a subject of strong debate in many Muslim countries. Sources of the *sharī'a* are the Qur'ān and the *sunna* (Muhammad's tradition, whose texts have given rise to many interpretations by the different juridical schools).

sheikh

The word itself means an old man, *sheik*, but in religious contexts, it is a title that means "elder" or "presbyter". It is also used in different Arab countries as an aristocratic title.

Shiites

The word refers to *Shī'at 'Alī* (the party of Ali). Ali was Muhammad's cousin and son-in-law and Fatima's husband. The Shiites were the protagonists of the first division inside Islam, due to the fight for the succession that followed Muhammad's death. The Shiites represent about 10 percent of Muslims. They live mainly in Iran, Pakistan, Iraq, Lebanon, and other Gulf countries.

shūra

Consultation. It is a name given to the legislative or advisory counsel in Islamic political systems.

Sīra

Muhammad's biography. The most authoritative is the one written by Ibn Hishām in the ninth century.

sunna

The Islamic traditions connected to Muhammad.

Sunni

He who follows the *sunna*. As a group, Sunnis represent 90 percent of Muslims in the world and are divided into four "rites", or schools: the Ḥanafi, related to Abū Ḥanīfa (700–768), widespread in Turkey, Egypt, Syria, Iraq, Pakistan, Afghanistan, and India; the Māliki, named after Mālik bin Anas (712–796), widespread in Maghreb and in black Africa; the Shāfi'i of *imām* Shāfi'ī (768–820), widespread in eastern Africa, south Arabia, and Indonesia; and the Ḥanbali of Ibn Ḥanbal (780–855) of Saudi Arabia, which produced the rigid Wahhabi doctrine of the royal family in Riyadh.

sura
A chapter of the Qur'ān. There are 114 chapters divided into Meccan and Medina suras.

tafsīr
The discipline of commenting on the Qur'ān. The commentator is called the *mufassir.*

tawḥīd
The Oneness, meaning the faith in the only God.

ta'wīl
The interpretation of the Qur'ān.

ʿulemā'
From the Arabic *ʿulemā'* (wise men, scholars). In the Muslim tradition, it refers to the qur'ānic "doctors of the law" who are in charge of interpreting the *sharīʿa.*

umma
Nation. Generally it is understood as the community to which all Muslims belong.

Wahhabi
Referring to the group that adopts the official doctrine in force in Saudi Arabia and that recalls the teaching of the theologian Muhammad bin ʿAbdil-Wahhāb (1703–1787). In the former Soviet Union, the word commonly indicates all the Islamic fundamentalist groups.

zakāt
Alms, a sort of tithe taken from earnings and used for charity. It is the third pillar of Islam.

Bibliography

Allievi, Stefano, and Jorgen S. Nielsen, eds. *Muslim Networks and Transnational Communities in and Across Europe.* Boston: Brill Academic Publishers, 2003.

Aluffi B.-P., Roberta, and Giovanna Zincone, eds. *The Legal Treatment of Islamic Minorities in Europe.* Leuven, Belgium: Peeters, 2004.

Belloc, Hilaire. *The Crusades: The World's Debate.* Rockford, Ill.: TAN Books, 1992.

Dashti, 'Ali. *23 Years: A Study of the Prophetic Career of Mohammad.* Costa Mesa, Calif.: Mazda Publishers, 1994.

Davis, Gregory M. *Religion of Peace? Islam's War Against the World.* Los Angeles: World Ahead Publishing, Inc., 2006.

Farah, Caesar E. *Islam: Beliefs and Observances.* 7th ed. Hauppauge, NY: Barron's, 2003.

Ferrari, Silvio, and Anthony Bradney, eds. *Islam and European Legal Systems.* Burlington, Vt.: Ashgate Publishing, 2000.

Fregosi, Paul. *Jihad in the West: Muslim Conquests from the 7th to the 21st Centuries.* New York: Prometheus Books, 1998.

Gardet, Louis. *Mohammedanism.* Translated by William Burridge. New York: Hawthorn Books, 1961.

Gordon, Matthew. *Islam: Origins, Practices, Holy Texts, Sacred Persons, Sacred Places*. Oxford, New York: Oxford University Press, 2002.

Guillaume, Alfred, trans. *The Life of Muhammad: A Translation of Ibn Ishaq's Sirat Rasul Allah*. New York: Oxford University Press, 2004.

Gulevich, Tanya. *Understanding Islam and Muslim Traditions: An Introduction to the Religious Practices, Celebrations, Festivals, Observances, Beliefs, Folklore, Customs, and Calendar System of the World's Muslim Communities, Including an Overview of Islamic History and Geography*. Detroit: Omnigraphics, 2004.

Hawting, G. R. *The idea of idolatry and the emergence of Islam: From Polemic to History*. Cambridge: Cambridge University Press, 1999

Hiskett, Mervyn. *Some to Mecca Turn to Pray*. St. Alban's: Claridge Press, 1993.

Hoyland, Robert G. *Seeing Islam As Others Saw It: A Survey and Evaluation of Christian, Jewish and Zoroastrian Writings on Early Islam*. Studies in Late Antiquity and Early Islam 13. Princeton: Darwin Press, 1997.

Huff, Toby E. *The Rise of Early Modern Science: Islam, China and the West*. 2nd ed. Cambridge: Cambridge University Press, 2003.

Israeli, Raphael. *Islamikaze: Manifestations of Islamic Martyrology*. London: Frand Cass Publishers, 2003.

Jomier, Jacques. *The Bible and the Qur'an*. Translated by Edward Arbez. San Francisco: Ignatius Press, 2002.

Kepel, Gilles. *Allah in the West: Islamic Movements in America and Europe*. Stanford: Stanford University Press, 1997.

Kepel, Gilles. *The Roots of Radical Islam*. London: Saqi, 2005.

Köse, Ali. *Conversion to Islam: A Study of Native British Converts*. New York: Kegan Paul International, 1996.

Lewis, Bernard. *Islam and the West*. New York: Oxford University Press, 1993.

Lewis, Bernard. *The Crisis of Islam: Holy War and Unholy Terror*. New York: Random House, 2004.

Lippman, Thomas W. *Understanding Islam: An Introduction to the Muslim World*. New York: Penguin Putnam, 2002.

Madden, Thomas F. *The New Concise History of the Crusades*. Lanham, Md.: Rowman & Littlefield, 2005.

Mallon, Elias D. *Islam: What Catholics need to know*. Washington, D.C.: National Catholic Educational Association, 2006.

Mantran, Robert, ed. *Great Dates in Islamic History*. New York: Facts on File, 1996.

McAuliffe, Jane Dammen, ed. *Encyclopaedia of Qur'an*. 1st ed., 5 vols. Leiden: Brill Publishers, 2001–2006.

Miller, John, and Aaron Kenedi, eds. *Inside Islam: The Faith, the People, and the Conflicts of the World's Fastest-growing Religion*. New York: Marlowe & Co., 2002.

Nanji, Azim A. *The Muslim Almanac: A Reference Work on the History, Faith, Culture, and Peoples of Islam*. Detroit: Gale Research, 1996.

Nasr, Seyyed Hossein. *Islamic Life and Thought*. Albany: State University of New York Press, 1981.

Nigosian, Solomon Alexander. *Islam: Its History, Teaching, and Practices*. Bloomington: Indiana University Press, 2004.

Péroncel-Hugoz, Jean-Pierre. *The Raft of Mohammed*. St. Paul: Paragon House, 1988.

Pontifical Council for Interreligious Dialogue, and Maurice Bormans. *Guidelines for Dialogues between Christians and Muslims*. Translated by R. Marston Speight. Mahwah, N.J.: Paulist Press, 1990.

Poston, Larry. *Islamic Da'wah in the West: Muslim Missionary Activity and the Dynamics of Conversion in Islam*. New York: Oxford University Press, 1992.

Qutb, Sayyid. *Islam and Universal Peace*. Plainfield, IN: American Trust Publications, 1993.

Qutb, Sayyid. *Milestones*. Chicago: Kazi Publications, 2003.

Ruthven, Malise. *Islam in the World*. 2nd ed. New York: Oxford University Press, 2000.

Schacht, Joseph. *An Introduction to Islamic Law*. New York: Clarendon Press, 1983.

Shorter Encyclopaedia of Islam. Leiden: Brill Publishers, 1953.

Spencer, Robert, ed. *The Myth of Islamic Tolerance: How Islamic Law Treats Non-Muslims*. Amherst, NY: Prometheus Books, 2005.

Spencer, Robert. *The Politically Incorrect Guide to Islam (And The Crusades)*. Washington D.C.: Regnery Publishing, 2005.

Spencer, Robert. *The Truth About Muhammad: Founder of the World's Most Intolerant Religion*. Washington, D.C.: Regnery Publishing, 2006.

Waines, David. *An Introduction to Islam*. Cambridge: Cambridge University Press, 2003.

Wansbrough, John. *Quranic Studies: Sources and Methods of Scriptural Interpretation*. London Oriental Series, vol. 31. Oxford: Oxford University Press, 1977.

Wansbrough, John. *The Sectarian Milieu: Content and Composition of Islamic Salvation History*. London Oriental Series, vol. 34. Oxford: Oxford University Press, 1978.

Warraq, Ibn, ed. *The Origins of The Koran: Classic Essays on Islam's Holy Book*. Amherst, N.Y.: Prometheus Books, 1998.

Warraq, Ibn. *The Quest for the Historical Muhammad*. Amherst, N.Y.: Prometheus Books, 2000.

Watt, William Montgomery. *Islam: A Short History*. Oxford: Oneworld, 1996.

Watt, William Montgomery. *Muhammad: Prophet and Statesman*. Oxford: Oxford University Press, 1961.

Zepp, Ira G. *A Muslim primer: beginner's guide to Islam*. Fayetteville: University of Arkansas Press, 2000.

Index

*Note: Page references in bold indicate
definitions.*

ḥurūb al-Faranj (the wars of the
Franks), 74
See also the Crusades; warfare
al-ḥurūb al-ṣalībiyya (Crusades),
74
husband rights, 110–19, 110n12,
113nn17–18, 114n20
See also rights
Ḥussein, King of Jordan, 186

Ibn Abī Ẓāhir, 73
Ibn Bādīs, 83
Ibn Ḥanbal, 69, 69n13, **238**
Ibn Hishām, 37, 37n9
Ibn Isḥāq, 37n9, **238**
Ibn Rushd, Abū al-Wālīd
Muḥammad (Averroes), 43,
43n22, 105
identity symbols, 114–16,
142–43, 169
Ignatius of Antioch, 204
iʿjāz (miracle), 47–48, **234**
See also miracles
ijmāʾ (consensus), 61
al-Ikhwān al-Muslimūn (Muslim
Brotherhood), 84–87, 102,
141–43, 148, 186, 228
immigrants/immigration
as challenge to Christians,
210–12
children, 116–17, 157–58
genders, 116–20, 155, 227–28
integration of Muslim, 142,
154–58, 161, 164–65, 167,
172–76
second and third generations
of, 146, 154–55, 228
See also integration of Muslims;
Islamization process
India, 83, 178, 178n2

Indonesia, 122–23nn25–26, 138
inequalities, social
Christianity on, 106–9,
123–24, 196, 202
husband rights, 110–19,
110n12, 113nn17–18,
114n20
inheritance and, 91, 97,
112–13, 112n16, 118, 165
polygamy and, 40n15, 79, 91,
97, 110, 165
religious freedom and, 95–99,
121–24, 127, 130–36, 144,
157, 210–11
sharīʿa and, 91
slavery and, 41, 79, 91, 114
testimony and, 112–13,
112n16, 121
women as inferior, 106–9,
107–8n10, 112–15, 196,
202
See also interpretation of
Qurʾān; rights; women
infanticide, 32
infibulation, 60
infidels. *See kāfir*
inheritance, 91, 97, 112–13,
112n16, 118, 165
integration of Muslims
immigrants/immigration and,
142, 154–58, 161, 164–65,
167, 172–76
models of, 172–76
multiculturalism, 144, 157–60,
173–75
non-literalist interpretations
and, 96–101, 131
parallel community vs.,
143–45, 147–48, 154–58,
160–67
See also dialogue